ON JUNE 21, 1861 nine full-blooded Dakotas applied for United States citizen-
ship at the U.S. district court in Mankato, and were with a single exception refused.
The rejection was based upon the fact that they could not speak English. One of
the Dakotas, upon return to his home near Yellow Medicine, told a white friend:

> They did not make us citizens, and we came home
> ashamed....I am an old man now, and I will never
> be made a citizen. We were bitterly opposed down
> there. One man made me feel very angry. He said
> that men with colored skin should never be natural-
> ized--that they could not be made white men.
>   What if the skin is white? If the actions are wicked,
> the soul is black; and though the skin is black, if God
> cleanse the soul, it is white. God made all men of one
> blood, and though a man have a dark skin, he is a man.
>   They treat us like dogs and I do not like it. I
> am greatly ashamed ever since I returned.

Source: *St. Peter Tribune*, July 10, 1861.

LITTLE CROW (TAOYATEDUTA)

DAKOTA ORATORY

GREAT MOMENTS IN THE RECORDED SPEECH OF THE
EASTERN SIOUX, 1695-1874

COMPILED AND ILLUSTRATED BY

Mark Diedrich

coyote books

ROCHESTER, MINNESOTA

"If you had continued with us, my dear son, how well would the bow have become your hand, and how fatal would your arrows have proved to the enemies of our bands. You would often have drank their blood, and eaten their flesh, and numerous slaves would have rewarded your toils. With a nervous arm would you have seized the wounded buffalo, or have combated the fury of the enraged bear. You would have overtaken the flying elk, and kept pace on the mountain's brow with the fleetest deer. What feats you might have performed had you stayed among us till age had given you strength, and your father had instructed you in every Indian accomplishment."

Speech, in substance, of a Dakota woman mourning for the loss of her young son, ca. 1767

Other books by Mark Diedrich:

The Chiefs Hole-in-the-Day of the
    Mississippi Chippewa (1986)
Famous Chiefs of the Eastern Sioux (1987)
The Odyssey of Chief Standing Buffalo
    and the Northern Sisseton Sioux (1988)

Cover illustration: "Red Owl," by Mark Diedrich, 1988
Frontispiece: "Little Crow," by Mark Diedrich, 1988

Contents

* * * * *

ILLUSTRATIONS BY MARK DIEDRICH:

Introduction

"The Great Spirit made all things. We lay our hands upon the sacred writings and appeal to the Great Spirit to bear witness that we speak the truth."
Red Iron, 1853

ALTHOUGH several historical and biographical studies have been written about the Eastern Dakota, or Sioux, people, little space has been found for Indian speeches. Indeed, historians must synthesize and interpret a vast amount of information, ironically, often at the expense of what the Dakotas themselves have said in their addresses and remarks. This volume therefore is devoted to the recorded speeches of the Dakotas and the stories and situations surrounding them. It differs from other publications of American Indian speeches in that it covers only the Eastern Dakota tribes--the Mantantons, the Mdewakantons, the Sissetons, the Wahpekutes, and the Wahpetons--a people who for hundreds of years, up until the mid-1800s, had claimed ownership of much of present-day Minnesota, western Wisconsin, Iowa, and eastern North and South Dakota. To a notable degree, this collection is a history of the Dakotas "in their own words." However, the reader will not only find remarks in regard to specific historical events, but also gain a sense of Dakota culture and religion. Indeed, poignant statements have been made in regard to the everyday issues of life, both great and small--war and peace, loyalty and betrayal, defeat and victory, traditional ways and Christianity, negotiation and confrontation, wealth and poverty, joy and despair, life and death.

Oratorical ability was of great importance to American Indian leaders, and the Dakotas were certainly no exception. In his recent history of the Eastern Dakota, Gary C. Anderson states that "concensus government" was "the hallmark of the Dakota political system" --therefore, good speakers were particularly influential members of their bands and tribes. Samuel W. Pond, who was a missionary among the Dakotas from the 1830s, explains: "Speeches well made and well timed had a great influence over the minds of the Dakotas, and a few words fitly spoken often changed the purposes of the inhabitants of a whole village." It was noted that Dakota civil chiefs, who often obtained their office hereditarily, frequently had little influence if they could not speak well. Many of the great chiefly lineages, however, did produce excellent orators--the Wabashas, Shakopees, and Little Crows in particular. Yet, from the 1830s onward, due to increasing political, cultural, and economic pressures, civil chiefs steadily lost influence, regardless of their speaking ability, and concensus among their bands and tribes grew increasingly more difficult to achieve. By the late 1840s it seems that, in order to arrive at greater political unity, especially in dealing with the U. S. government, the Mdewakanton Dakota instituted the office of "chief speaker" --a position to which they elected their most prominent orators. Bad Hail, Little Crow (Taoyateduta), and Traveling Hail are known to have served in this capacity; and Little Paul Mazakutemani was given a corresponding office by the Wahpetons and Sissetons in the late 1850s. By that time, the Dakota political system was complicated even further by the rise of Soldiers' Lodge institutions in which young men elected their own speakers. Red Owl and Rattling Runner were outstanding examples of these.

Of the speeches themselves, Pond felt that overall they were "more remarkable for spirit and force than for smoothness and elegance." He thought that the poorest speeches were made in council with whites as the speakers often felt compelled to solicit presents and "their begging spoiled their speeches." He concluded that "the best addresses of Indian orators must have been made under circumstances that few white men were likely to hear them or hear of them." While this may be true, it is certain that the body of speeches made before whites was of great importance to the Dakotas, as well as an obvious necessity, and that they doubtless wanted to be accurately and eloquently represented by their orators. Thus, it would be reasonable to assume that the speeches recorded by the whites would have the same general tenor as the mass of unrecorded speeches made among the Indians themselves.

In considering the speeches, it is also necessary to admit that interpretation is a great vagary. Historian Herman J. Viola has commented on the problem: "Since almost all the statements purporting to be direct quotations [from Indians] were obtained through interpreters, one has to question whether [these] accounts were the product of the [Indians]..., the interpreters, or the reporters." Many of the interpreters for the Dakotas were people of mixed-blood, who spoke Dakota fluently, but yet had minimal education in the English language. Due to this handicap, they often reported only the substance of the Indian speeches; Pond said that "if the Dakotas had understood English they would have hardly recognized their own speeches." Several speeches of this type are included in this volume because they were very important--this is regretable, but obviously inevitable. A Washington reporter complained in 1858 of a "substance only" translation of a speech by Little Crow (given by Joseph Brown): the chief "delivered this harangue with expressive gesticulation and there was much regret that his own language was not understood." On the other hand, interpreters often had to convey English spoken by highly educated whites to the Dakotas. Even if they fully understood all that was spoken to them, they also faced the problem that the English language had more words than the Dakota. George Spencer, a trader among the Dakotas in the 1860s, went so far as to state: "It is my opinion that more than one-half of the misunderstandings which have arisen between the Indians and the government may be traced to the fact that the interpreter did not understand, himself, what had been said to him." Yet, despite the aforementioned qualifications, it is well to note that several interpreters had long experience in their jobs and probably did them very adequately. Scott Campbell, although a mixed-blood, served as government interpreter for Agent Lawrence Taliaferro for some twenty years. And another long time and often used interpreter was Philander Prescott, an educated white descended from the famous Prescotts of New England. At any rate, what was lost in the translation and interpretation of the speeches cannot now be determined or rectified.

The recording of the speeches is the next main problem. Again, it is impossible to tell what has been lost or twisted or restated in the writing down of Indian speeches. Speeches were noted by agents, missionaries, treaty recorders, travelers, explorers, and reporters for newspapers. Sometimes the Dakotas themselves had their speeches written down as letters. Dakota agent Lawrence Taliaferro was perhaps the most prolific recorder of Indian speech; his journals contain a great amount of material to choose from for a volume such as this--however, this had to be limited in order to round out this book chronologically (as well as from a source standpoint). Numerous speeches were also recorded during specific events such as the treaty councils of 1837, 1851, and 1858--yet many of these kind of speeches were quite repetitive, and not all Dakota leaders had much to say, or were not able to speak for any length of time. Of course, the war in Minnesota in 1862 generated many speeches, and because of the significance of the war, many speeches were recorded--this is reflected by the space given to these in this volume.

Lastly, of the approximately eighty speeches herein, the majority were given by members of the Mdewakanton Dakota. This indicates the fact that this tribe was the most prominent in affairs with the whites, particularly during the period of time when most of the speeches were recorded--1812 through 1862. Of the forty or so individual speakers, the Mdewakanton chief, Little Crow (Taoyateduta) has been given the most space; he is undoubtedly the most famous orator in the history of the Eastern Dakota. (See the appendices for lists of the Dakota speakers and their interpreters.)

Mark Diedrich

WABASHA (II)

MARK DIEDRICH 1987

CHAPTER ONE

THE FRENCH and BRITISH PERIOD, 1695-1816

"I am a bastard in quest of a father."

"I am a bastard in quest of a father...."

TIYOSKATE   July 18, 1695

THE DAKOTA, OR SIOUX, TRIBES had lived in central Minnesota for several hundred years when they first came into contact with French explorers. On July 2, 1679 Daniel Greysolon, or Sieur Du Luth, visited the Dakota villages at Mille Lacs and claimed the land for the King of France. From this early period, the Dakota began to consider, or at least characterize, themselves as "children" who needed the protection of a "great father"--such as the French King, who could supply them with "iron"--or the guns which the Frenchmen carried which were so far superior to Dakota stone age weapons. As the fur trade was the means by which they could gain these guns, they considered it a matter of national importance that French traders be sent among them. In fact, the Dakotas soon equated trade with "life" itself.

The leading Dakota tribe of the late seventeenth century was the Mantanton. They migrated south from the Onamia Lake area to the mouth of the Minnesota River in the 1680s in order to avail themselves of a French trading post on Prairie Island near the head of Lake Pepin. In 1695 the Mantanton chief, Tiyoskate, persuaded Pierre Charles LeSueur to take him to Montreal to meet Frontenac, the governor general of New France. The chief intended to pledge Dakota allegiance to the French King, beg for trade, and ask aid for recovering people who had been taken captive by other tribes.

On July 18, 1695, the forty-year-old chief received his audience with Frontenac. He presented a beaver robe, an otter skin, and a tobacco pouch, and then proceeded to weep bitterly--as was the Dakota custom at the time, when about to speak of matters of grave importance. He explained that all of the Indian nations (to the east) had a father who protected them and gave them "iron," but that he was "a bastard in quest of a father." He then placed twenty-two arrows on the beaver robe and said that they represented twenty-two Dakota villages which desired French protection. Continuing, he said:

> It is not on account of what I bring that I hope he who
> rules this earth will have pity on me. I learned from the
> Sauters [or People of the Sault Ste. Marie--the Ojibway,
> or Chippewa] that he wanted nothing; that he was the
> Master of Iron; that he had a big heart into which he
> could receive all the nations. This has induced me to
> abandon my people to come to seek his protection, and
> to beseech him to receive me among the number of his
> children. Take courage great captain, and reject me not;
> despise me not, though I appear poor in your eyes. All
> the nations here present know that I am rich, and the
> little they offer here is taken from my lands.

Frontenac promised to receive the Dakotas if they would be obedient to the French. The chief replied joyfully that the governor had just restored his tribe "to life by promising to send them iron." Unfortunately, Tiyoskate fell ill and died; he was buried in a Montreal cemetery on February 3, 1696. One hundred and fifty years later, Stephen Riggs heard this chief spoken of by his descendants.

Sources: Newton D. Winchell, *The Aborigines of Minnesota* (St. Paul: Minnesota Historical Society, 1911), 527-28; Emma H. Blair, ed. *The Indian Tribes of the Upper Mississippi Valley....*, 2 vols. (Cleveland: Arthur H. Clark, Co., 1911), 2:109-31.

"...in a little time, the Mantantons will become Frenchmen."

WAKANTAPI   December 1, 1700

AFTER THE DEATH OF TIYOSKATE, Wakantapi became the head chief of the Mantantons. It became his task to see that tribal relations with the French went smoothly so that trade would not be withheld from them. Such a disruption almost occurred in the fall of 1700 after the Mdewakantons of Mille Lacs robbed a French trader. LeSueur, who was then operating out of a fort at the mouth of the Blue Earth River, immediately threatened to cut off trade goods from the Mantantons. Wakantapi, along with other relatives of the deceased Tiyoskate, visited LeSueur, with their faces painted black (a Dakota custom when in mourning), and wept for a period of fifteen minutes. Then, the chief asked the trader to pity them and supply them with powder and balls that they might defend themselves against their enemies (who had been slaughtering them of late) and gain a living by hunting. LeSueur granted the request, and the grateful chief planned a great feast for the Frenchmen two weeks later. On that occasion, LeSueur invited the Mantantons to live near his fort where they would be "shielded from the insults of their enemies" and he could help them to raise corn. In reply, Wakantapi smoked from his hatchet pipe--passed it around, gave LeSueur a slave (undoubtedly a member of an enemy tribe) and a bag of wild rice, and said:

> Behold the remains of this great village, which you have aforetimes seen so numerous! All the others have been killed in war, and the few men you see in this lodge accept the present you have made them, and are resolved to obey the great chief of all nations, of whom you have spoken to us.
>
> You ought not to regard us as Sioux, but as French, and instead of saying the Sioux are miserable, and have no mind, and are fit for nothing but to rob and steal from the French, you shall say "my brothers are miserable and have no mind, and we must try to procure some for them. They rob us, but I will take care that they do not lack iron, that is to say, all kinds of goods." If you do this, I assure you that in a little time the Mantantons will become Frenchmen, and they will have none of those vices with which you reproach us.

The plans of Wakantapi and LeSueur, however, were both frustrated. In the spring of 1701 LeSueur returned to France with half of his men; the remaining Frenchmen left the following year. Trade with the French was completely disrupted due to the Queen Anne War between France and England (1702-1713). French traders did not return to Mantanton country until 1726, when Fort Beauharnois was established near Lake Pepin. Then, due to Dakota wars with the Chippewa, and Dakota hostility against the French, trade continued only erratically. Soon the Dakotas would have to deal with a new "great father" from Great Britain.

Source: Edward D. Neill, "Le Seur, the Explorer of the Minnesota River," *Minnesota Historical Collections*, 1 (1872):328-35.

"And may peace subsist between us, so long as the sun, the moon, the earth, and the waters shall endure."

MANTANTON CHIEF   May 1, 1767

IN 1755 THE FRENCH and their Indian allies began fighting the British for domination of North America. The war was ended in 1763 when the French government signed the Treaty of Paris and ceded to Great Britain all of her possessions in Canada and on the continent east of the Mississippi. Although the Dakotas were not involved, many of the Great Lakes tribes resisted the British occupation of their lands in the Pontiac War, but they were defeated. The Dakotas had already decided to ally themselves to the victorious English King. A number of warriors, including perhaps the great Dakota war chief, Wabasha I, visited Fort Edward at Green Bay on March 1, 1763; they said that "if ever the Chippewas or any other Indians wished to obstruct passage of traders coming up, to send them word, and they would come and put them off the face of the earth, as all Indians were their slaves or dogs." In the fall of 1766 Captain Jonathan Carver visited the Mantanton and Mdewakanton bands on the Mississippi. He encouraged them to give their allegiance to the British King and was answered by a hereditary chief of the Mantantons:

> Good brother! I am now about to speak to you with the mouths of these my brothers, chiefs of the eight bands of the powerful nation of the Naudowessies [or Sioux]. We believe and are well satisfied in the truth of every thing you have told us about your great nation, and the Great King, our greatest father, for whom we spread this beaver blanket, that his fatherly protection may ever rest easy and safe among us, his children: your colors and your arms agree with the accounts you have given us about your great nation. We desire that when you return, you will acquaint the Great King how much the Naudowessies wish to be counted among his good children. You may believe us when we tell you that we will not open our ears to any who may dare to speak evil of our Great Father, the King of the English and other nations.
>   We thank you for what you have done for us in making peace between the Naudowessies and the Chippewas, and hope that when you return to us again, that you will complete this good work; and quite dispelling the clouds that intervene, open the blue sky of peace, and cause the bloody hatchet to be deep buried under the roots of the great tree of peace.
>   We wish you to remember to represent to our Great Father, how much we desire that traders may be sent to abide among us, with such things as we need, that the hearts of our young men, our wives, and children may be made glad. And may peace subsist between us, so long as the sun, the moon, the earth, and the waters shall endure. Farewell.

Peace did prevail between the Dakotas and the English, however, the British colonists to the east became involved in the American Revolutionary War. The British sought help and received military aid from Dakota warriors led by the pre-eminent war chief, Wabasha, who was made a British "general." They assisted in a campaign against the Spanish and Americans at St. Louis, but the war soon after ended in 1783. The Americans, known as the "Long Knives" to the Indians, gained title to the land east of the Mississippi, including some which the Dakotas considered their own. The Sioux were now faced with the uneasy question as to how an American "great father" would treat them.

Source: Jonathan Carver, *Travels Through the Interior Parts of North America in the Years 1766, 1767, 1768* (Minneapolis: Ross and Haines, Inc., 1956), 63-91.

"...I will blow you from the face of the earth...."

WABASHA II   1812

WABASHA (RED STANDARD) succeeded his renowned father as chief of the Kiuksa band of the Mdewakanton Dakota by about 1800. He was early accorded the title of first chief of his tribe and of the eastern Dakotas generally. Few chiefs ever displayed a more dignified air. The Italian count, Beltrami, described the chief in the 1820s: "...though wrapped in a wretched buffalo's skin, [he] had perfectly the air and aspect of a man of quality. His countenance, his arched eyebrows, his large nose, which he blew with great noise though without a handkerchief, the motion of his right hand, with which he frequently stroked his forehead and chin, his thoughtful air, his eyes fixed as if entranced, and his imposing manner of sitting, although on the ground, all marked him for a great statesman...." The chief was indeed a great statesman, although he was not as inclined to war as his father.

On one occasion in 1812, it was said that the white community at Prairie du Chien was being harassed by the Winnebago tribe, and that they turned to Wabasha for protection. As some of the whites had married into his family, the chief felt obliged to mediate the situation: he called a council with the Winnebago leaders. Then, according to Mary Eastman's account, Wabasha "arose and looked upon the chiefs with a menacing look. His countenance was fierce and terrible; and cold and stern were the faces upon which his piercing eye was bent. He plucked a single hair from his head, held it up before them, and then spoke in a grave and resolute tone":

> Winnebagoes, do you see this hair? Look at it. You threaten to massacre the white people at the prairie. They are your friends and mine. You wish to drink their blood. Is that your purpose? Dare to lay a finger upon one of them, and I will blow you from the face of the earth, as I now blow this hair with my breath where none can find it.

Eastman continues: "Not a word was uttered, not a look expressed an intention of differing from him, and Wabashaw, with a look of proud defiance, left the council...."

Sources: Giacomo C. Beltrami, *A Pilgrimage in America*, 2 vols. (London: Hunt and Clarke, 1828), 2:181; Mary H. Eastman, *The American Aboriginal Portfolio* (Philadelphia: Lippincott, Grambo and Co., 1853), 82. Very few speeches given by Wabasha I were ever recorded--two that were can be found in Mark Diedrich, *Famous Chiefs of the Eastern Sioux* (Minneapolis: Coyote Books, 1987), 3, 10.

"We abandon forever any connection with the Liars...."

WABASHA, PETIT CORBEAU, and RED WING   June 10, 1812

IN EARLY JUNE 1812, Robert Dickson, the leading British trader on the upper Mississippi, sent word to the chiefs of the Mdewakanton Dakota to come for an urgent council at Prairie du Chien. He said that war was expected to break out soon with the "Long Knives"--the Americans, and that Lieutenant Governor Isaac Brock had sent him to procure their help in putting down their common enemy. Because the Mdewakantons had been for a long time supplied by English traders, particularly Dickson and his associates, the chiefs were eager to prove their loyalty to the English. Wabasha replied first:

> We live by our English traders, who had always assisted us, and never more so than this last year, at the risk of their lives, and we are at all times ready to listen to them on account of the friendship they have always shown us. From the last band of our nation to the west, we hold each other's hands. We have some here fortunately, because we have this day met the words of our English Father. They are such as we would wish and expect; at all times we are ready to follow his advice, and now more so than ever. We have always found our English Father the protector of our women and children, but we have for some time past been amused by the songs of bad birds from the lower part of the river--they were not the songs of truth, and this day we rejoice in again hearing the voice of our English Father, who never deceived us, and we are certain never will.

Petit Corbeau, or Little Crow, the second ranking chief of the Mdewakantons, and a leading war chief, was next to speak:

> My friend who has just spoken has uttered the truth. The voice I have just heard from our English Father is as if one was raised from the dead and restored to his friends. From our ancestors we have learned the generous conduct of the English to all nations. The evil voice of bad birds has for some time past interrupted our communications with those we love. We are now fully convinced of the falsity of their dealing. Although unacquainted with the acts of white people, we know the truth of Englishmen, and as a proof of it this day, we take up the pipes from deceased friends to be a testimony to the truth of our words.

Red Wing (or Walking Buffalo--Tatankamani), another great band and war chief, added:

> How can we savages be instructed without listening to the voice of those who have never deceived us. We remember the words of our ancestors; we were then accustomed to live more at our ease, than we have done for some time past; but we have been deceived by liars. We rejoice today at being again on the road to the chief who has conferred so many benefits on our nation. We abandon forever any connection with the liars, who have uniformly deceived us....

Source: Robert Dickson to British Officer at Fort George, June 10, 1812, Robert Dickson Papers, Minnesota Historical Society.

"...we came here, not to eat Americans, but to wage war against them...."

PETIT CORBEAU   1813

IN THE SUMMER OF 1813 a contingent of Dakota warriors and chiefs joined the British forces under General Henry Proctor for a campaign against the Americans. They beseiged Fort Miegs on the Maumee River (near present day Toledo, Ohio), which was commanded by American General William H. Harrison.

During the bombardment, Petit Corbeau, his nephew Big Hunter, and His Bow, were invited to an Indian council. Accompanied by their interpreter, Captain Joseph Renville, they arrived in time to witness the cutting up and apportioning of the body of an American soldier into dishes with corn. The bravest man of each tribe present was called upon to eat a portion of the head and heart! Little Crow's nephew was asked to have a share in these "special parts." At that point Petit Corbeau interrupted the proceedings, and sending his nephew away, said:

> **My friends, we came here, not to eat Americans, but to wage war against them; that will suffice for us; and could we even do that if left to our own forces. We are poor and destitute, while they possess the means of supplying themselves with all that they require; we ought not therefore to do such things.**

His Bow (Wabasha's nephew) added: "We thought that you, who live near to the white men, were wiser and more refined than we are, who live at a distance; but it must indeed be otherwise if you do such deeds." The Winnebago who originated the feast later told Colonel Dickson that it was "better for him to kill the American and eat him, than it was for the Americans to burn his house, ravish and murder his wife and daughters."

Source: William H. Keating, *Narrative of an Expedition to the Source of St. Peter's River* (Minneapolis: Ross and Haines, Inc., 1959), 1:394-96. It is interesting to note that, although the eastern Dakotas did not practice any form of cannibalism usually, the renowned medicine man and war partisan, Tamaha, admitted to having eaten of a Chippewa body; he spoke of it "without repugnance," and said that he found the breast meat to be the most delicate. Keating, ibid, 1:414n.

"The living brave betrays no trust."

TAMAHA   1814

TAMAHA was one of the remarkable individuals of the Mdewakanton Dakota whose life spanned over one hundred years--his birth predated the earliest British explorations of the northwest, and before his death he saw the complete removal of his tribe from their Minnesota homelands. He was noted for his particular friendship with Lieutenant Zebulon Pike, and his role in the War of 1812, during which he served the American cause.

American Colonel William Clark was happy to accept Tamaha's services, and aware of his influence as an orator, entrusted him with a mission in 1813 to persuade the Teton Dakotas of the Missouri River to remain faithful to the Americans. Successful in this venture, Tamaha journeyed as far as the Ohio country to spread rumors among his pro-British countrymen, that the Tetons were going to make war on the defenseless eastern Dakota villages. As a result, most of the Dakotas immediately left for home. In 1814, however, Tamaha was taken into custody by Colonel Dickson at Prairie du Chien. He was ordered to deliver up all communications from Colonel Clark on the threat of death. Unmoved, the determined war chief replied:

> Tamaha is a good Indian. He has no fear of death. He told his white chief, Governor Clark, that he would carry his talk to his people at Prairie du Chien. He had endeavored to do so. He was a prisoner of war. He could do no more. This and only this made the heart of Tamaha sad.
> Tamaha has no secrets to reveal to Colonel Dickson. The talk of his white chief to Tamaha should be buried with Tamaha in the silent earth. Why should Colonel Dickson kill Tamaha? What would he gain? The dead tell no tales. The living brave betrays no trust.
> Colonel Dickson, the heart of Tamaha is strong. If one word would save the life of Tamaha, Tamaha would not speak that word to save his life. As the forest leaf falls silently and calmly to the ground, so shall Tamaha go calmly and silently to the spirit land. The talk of Tamaha is ended.

Dickson, who was married to a Dakota woman and had spent many years among the Dakota tribes, decided against taking Tamaha's life. Instead, he released the persuasive war chief and told him to go back to St. Louis. The following spring, Tamaha came back upriver and achieved further notoriety by rescuing the American flag from the flames of the abandoned British fort at Prairie du Chien. Tamaha was given a hero's welcome in St. Louis.

Sources: Charles S. Bryant, "Incidents in the Life of Tarmaha, a Dakota Chief of the Red Wing band, now over 100 years Old," in the *Wabashaw Daily Journal*, May 5, 19, 26, June 2, 1860; *Missouri Gazette and Illinois Advertiser*, (St. Louis), June 17, 1815.

"I saw the future in my dreams three times...."

RED WING   1814

RED WING had been pro-British in June 1812, however, he soon changed his stance. This was due initially to his son's trip to Washington City with American agent Nicholas Boilvin to meet President James Madison. The chief was greatly impressed with the Americans' good treatment of his son. In addition to this, Red Wing was greatly influenced by his dreams, some of which were prophetic in nature. Seeing the future in his dreams had enabled him to become the greatest war chief of his tribe. His dreams also convinced him not to fight the Americans. He told British Captain Thomas Anderson of his decision:

> I have had another dream. You know all the blood in my heart is English; but I will not now fight the Big Knives. I have given to you my band and my children. They, with all the other Indians, are your soldiers, and will fight for you; but Red Wing will not raise his warclub. I saw the future in my dreams three times....
>
> You tell me that the lion on this [British] medal is the most powerful of all animals. I have never seen one, but I believe what you say. This lion, like our tiger, sleeps all day, but the eagle, who is the most powerful of birds, only sleeps at night; in the daytime he flies about everywhere, and sees all on the ground. He will light on a tree over the lion, and they will scold at each other for a while, but they will finally make up and be friends, and smoke the pipe of peace. The lion will then go home, and leave us Indians with our foes. That is the reason for not taking up my warclub. Your enemies will believe me when I speak good words to them.

Thus, Red Wing accurately foretold the outcome of the war: the English "lion" soon made peace with the American "eagle." The Dakotas were left to work out their own future with the victors. In the spring of 1815 Red Wing was among the first of the Dakota chiefs to travel to St. Louis to sign a treaty of peace.

Sources: Diedrich, *Famous Chiefs*, 20-21; Mark F. Diedrich, "Red Wing: War Chief of the Mdewakanton Dakota," *Minnesota Archaeologist*, 40 (March 1981):19-32.

"Will these presents pay for the men we have lost...?"

WABASHA and PETIT CORBEAU   June 1816

THE TREATY OF GHENT between Britain and the United States, which officially
ended the War of 1812, was signed on December 24, 1814; the news did not reach
Prairie du Chien, and the Dakotas, until late May 1815. The pro-British Dakota
chiefs were furious that they had not been consulted and began to worry about the
predicament the British were leaving them in with the Long Knives. Wabasha and
Petit Corbeau led a delegation of chiefs and warriors all the way to Drummond's
Island on Lake Huron in 1816 to have a last council with the British high command,
as represented by colonels McKay and McDouall. After the British explained the
peace with the Americans and brought forth presents for the tribes who had been
their allies, Wabasha spoke, with Joseph Renville interpreting:

> My father, what is this I see before me? A few knives
> and blankets! Is this all you promised at the beginning
> of the war? Where are those promises you made at
> Michilmackinac and sent to our villages on the Mississippi?
> You told us you would never let fall the hatchet until
> the Americans were driven out, that your king would
> never make peace without consulting us. You now say
> that this peace was made by your king without the
> knowledge of his war chiefs. What is this to us? Will
> these presents pay for the men we have lost, or make
> good your promises to us? For myself, I am an old man.
> I have lived long and have always found means of support
> and can do so still.

Petit Corbeau, considered by the British to be the first ranking war chief of the
eastern Dakotas, was even more outraged by the turn of events than his principal
chief, and added:

> Now, after we have fought for you, endured many
> hardships, lost some of our people, and awakened
> the vengeance of a powerful nation, our neighbors,
> you make a peace for yourselves, and leave us these
> goods as a compensation for having deserted us. But
> no! We will not take them; we hold them and your-
> selves in equal contempt!

Source: Doane Robinson, *A History of the Dakota or Sioux Indians* (Minneapolis: Ross and Haines Inc., 1956), 85, 100.
See also, Council, June 29, 1816, Robert Dickson Papers, Minnesota Historical Society (MHS). Colonel McDouall wrote
on June 19, 1816, after speaking with Petit Corbeau: "It is inconceivable the horror they entertain by the idea of the
English and their Traders being prohibited from going amongst them. The Little Corbeau, who frequently distinguished
himself in our cause during the late war, and who from his abilities takes a lead in Indian politics, told me this evening,
with much sensibility, that he considered this measure as sealing the ruin of the Indian nations and aiming at their
final extinction." R. McDouall to Secretary of War, June 19, 1816, Dickson Papers.

"...no one is to call me English any longer...."

WABASHA   August 20, 1816

AFTER HIS RETURN from Drummond's Island, by way of Mackinac, Wabasha had a council with American Colonel Willoughby Morgan at Fort Crawford, Prairie du Chien. On August 20, 1816 the chief delivered a speech which one historian has called "a masterpiece of diplomacy." The Americans had accused him of still being sympathetic to the British, and criticized him for being slow to come to councils with the Americans. Wabasha explained his position, probably with Joseph LaRocque (or Roc) interpreting:

> You wish to know what I did at Mackinac. I am going to say this to you: I have made my adieu to a father who has always treated me well and to say to him that he will never see me at his house, that I have taken another path and that I shall not leave it; they wished to give me fine clothes, a beautiful medal; and I sent everything back to them, saying, "I take this medal from my neck to put on another from another father. I do not know whether he will treat me as well as you. Keep your flag because it is fitting that another should flutter in my village."
>
> Thus have I made my adieu. They clothed all my warriors and chiefs, women and children, but as for me, I have come with this old garment. However, when any Englishman shall come to the post of my lodge, I shall open it up to him as you did.
>
> I am polite and hospitable at home. He did not speak to me at all of war. This is the result of my voyage to Mackinac....That is the reason that no one is to call me English any longer, since I gave my heart to the Americans. I should not wish to ask anything of you, since you bring nothing with you. You come nonetheless our friend. Some day our Great Father will recognize us and he will send us something....

Source: P. L. Scanlan, "Nicholas Boilvin, Indian Agent," *Wisconsin Magazine of History* (Dec. 1943), 27:158; Volumes 2 and 3, pp. 221-23, William Clark Papers, Kansas State Historical Society, Topeka.

PETIT CORBEAU
(CHETANWAKUAMANI)

MARK
DIEDRICH
1988

CHAPTER TWO

THE EARLY AMERICAN PERIOD, 1818-1837

"I see your people are well-dressed--we are obliged to wear skins."

"...we will gnaw them with our teeth."

SHAKOPEE   May 1818

SHAKOPEE, OR SIX, was born in about 1760 and was the son of a Shakopee before
him. At some point he became chief of the Prairie Village band of Mdewakantons
which camped on the Minnesota River, thirty-six miles from its mouth. He had joined
many of his fellow chiefs in serving the British in the War of 1812. The traders considered him an intelligent, but dishonest, man. In the spring of 1818 Shakopee was visited
at his village by a company of Dragoons led by Benjamin O'Fallon, the nephew of
William Clark. O'Fallon, whose mission was to keep the Dakotas from becoming dis-
affected from the Americans, commented: "this Six is one of the most daring,
ferocious, and savage looking fellows I have ever seen." Shakopee told O'Fallon
that a war party of Chippewas was heading towards the Dakota villages--he was fear-
ful that O'Fallon would try to prevent the Dakotas from warring with their enemies:

> American Chief! the Chippewas are coming upon us;
> we are not women, we must defend ourselves....The
> Big Knives have tied our hands; the American Chief
> whose place you have taken, told us we must not fight,
> but act as dutiful children, or incur the displeasure of
> the Big Knives.
>   We are no children. We are men, and had we such
> arms as your soldiers, who are standing before us, we
> would be valued as men. The Big Knives did wish to
> tie us like dogs under the hatchet of our enemies.
>   There was a time when we did awe the Chippewas
> within their proper limits but were unfortunately ordered
> to make peace. We did so--they presumed upon our
> obedience; they are coming upon us--look around and
> imagine that you hear the cries of our women and
> children, what must be the feeling of a bridled soldier--
> the most of our young men have disposed of their arms
> and ammunition. We have but little more than the gifts of
> nature to defend ourselves with. We will not submit.

O'Fallon surprised the chief greatly by saying that the Dakotas were justified in
defending themselves. Shakopee threw off his blanket and leggings and said joyfully:

> American Chief, my heart feels glad; look around
> and see the glistening countenances of my warriors--
> the sun, the heavens and the earth feel gay. We will
> follow your advice--[we] will leave a few of our soldiers
> to guard the women and children, and meet them in
> the plains, man to man--We will fight them--and those
> of my people who have no arms shall fight them with
> what nature has given them. Yes, we will scratch them
> with our toe and fingernails and we will gnaw them with
> our teeth.

Source: Benjamin O'Fallon to William Clark, May 20, 1818, in Clarence E. Carter, ed. *The Territorial Papers of
the United States* (Washington: Government Printing Office, 1951), 15:409-10.

"...we love our lands and the bones of our ancestors...."

DAKOTA HEADMEN   October 20, 1818

ALTHOUGH WABASHA and Red Wing returned to their Mississippi villages after
the close of the war, Petit Corbeau and many of his people went off to live near Lake
Traverse at the invitation of British traders. By the fall of 1818, however, most Dakotas
wished to return to their former villages. Among them were Petit Corbeau's nephew,
Big Hunter (Grand Chasseur), and his head soldier, Grand Partizan. They along with
several Sissetons of Traverse des Sioux wrote a letter to Nicholas Boilvin at
Prairie du Chien:

> Father...there came here a chief of the soldiers [O'Fallon]
> with an agent, who told us to remain quiet on our lands,
> until he could go down to St. Louis and return, and that
> he would supply all our wants....We believed, but he has
> done as the rest, he has deceived us; you see the injury
> that he had done us; we were in a state of starvation all
> last summer, seeing also that war had commenced by all
> the Indians who surrounded us....The British on Red
> River seized that moment to draw us over to Red River,
> and sent a trader...to draw us off, telling us that we would
> be always unhappy if we listened to the Americans.
>   Father, we will wait for your talk to decide; if it is
> your wish that we should remain on our lands, we will do
> so; if you wish that we should withdraw we will depart
> next spring....Remember we love our lands, and the bones
> of our ancestors that cover the prairie, and we wish to
> leave ours near theirs....
>   Father, you know some of our chiefs are feeble and
> love that strong water [whiskey] that makes men foolish
> and occasions them to do foolish things; it is that, that
> tempts them, seeing that the British had brought a large
> quantity of spiritous liquor; many of our people who
> were dry are gone to drink and receive what has been
> promised them at the settlements on Red River.
>   Father, if you love us yet, believe us we will bring
> to you all them people back next spring, if you will
> assist us by sending us a drop of that bad milk [whiskey]
> and a pipe of tobacco to talk to them, and we will show
> them, that, they must listen to their American Father;
> and [we] will make it appear that the milk that they get
> at Red River is sour in comparison to what we get here,
> which is pure and without poison....

The letter reveals to what extent liquor was dispensed as a present to persuade the
Dakotas to go here or there and be loyal to a certain group. Liquor had become
known by a term meaning mother's milk--thus representing the sense of loyalty
or obligation that a trader or diplomat may have wished to arouse in the Dakotas
or other tribes. Unfortunately, such prominent chiefs, like Petit Corbeau, became
alcoholics to varying degrees.

Sources: Sioux of Traverse des Sioux and Grand Marais to Nicholas Boilvin, Oct. 20, 1818, Thomas Forsyth
Papers, Missouri Historical Society, St. Louis; on the liquor trade, see Bruce M. White, "A Skilled Game of Exchange: Ojibway Fur Trade Protocol," *Minnesota History* (Summer 1987), 50:229-240.

"...this is war for land which must always exist...."

PETIT CORBEAU   August 1819

AFTER AN EXTENDED ABSENCE on the Red River, Petit Corbeau, chief of the old Mantanton tribal remnant, returned to his village site at Grand Marais; he had finally resigned himself to American dominance of the Upper Mississippi region. In August 1819 he witnessed the arrival of U.S. soldiers under Colonel Henry Leavenworth who were to begin military occupation at Mendota--on land which the old chief, himself, had granted to the Americans in his treaty with Zebulon Pike in 1805. Agent Thomas Forsyth, who had accompanied Leavenworth, spoke with Little Crow, and considered him a "steady, generous and independent Indian," who acknowledged the military reservation land sale. Learning that fifty of the chief's men were presently absent on a war party against the Chippewas, Forsyth, like previous agents, tried to persuade the chief to make peace. Petit Corbeau, probably with Duncan Campbell interpreting, replied:

> A peace could easily be made, but it is better for
> us to carry on the war in the way we do than to
> make peace, because we lose a man or two every
> year, but we kill as many of the enemy during the
> same time, and if we were to make peace, the Chip-
> pewas would overrun all the country lying between
> the Mississippi and Lake Superior, and have their
> villages on the banks of the Mississippi itself. In this
> case, we, the Sioux, would lose all our hunting
> grounds on the northeast side of the river; why then
> should we give up such an extensive country to save
> the life of a man or two annually? I know that it
> is not good to go to war, or to make too much war,
> or against too many people; but this is war for land
> which must always exist if the Dakota Indians
> remain in the same opinion which now guides them.

Forsyth commented in his journal that Little Crow's reasoning on the subject was so good that he spoke no more to him about it. Later, when the government sponsored peace councils between the tribes, the Dakotas frequently complained that their enemies had gained an advantage over them with consequent loss of hunting territory.

Source: Thomas Forsyth, "Journal of a Voyage from St. Louis to the Falls of St. Anthony, in 1819," *Wisconsin Historical Collections*, 6 (1872):213-17.

"I have taken our father here by the coattail...."

PETIT CORBEAU   1824

FIVE DAKOTA HEADMEN had journeyed to Washington City ("the seat of government") in 1812--the first time for any Dakota. Because the trip had fostered favorable pro-American sentiment, agent Nicholas Boilvin agitated for permission to bring the principal chiefs to Washington in 1816; however, the government declined at that time. But eight years later, in 1824, Lawrence Taliaferro, the Dakota agent, received permission to take a delegation to the capitol. Invitations were extended to such notable chiefs as Wabasha (II), Petit Corbeau, and Waneta (of the Yanktonai). Upon reaching Prairie du Chien, some consternation developed in the delegation as certain traders attempted to dissuade them from making the journey, saying that they would get sick and die. Petit Corbeau, however, boldly defended the trip:

> My friends, you can do as you please; I am no
> coward, nor can my ears be pulled about by
> evil counsels. We are here, and should go on and
> do some good for our nation. I have taken our
> father here by the coattail and will follow him
> into his great nation to see and take by the hand
> our great American Father. My mind is made up,
> live or die. (Turning to the agent and shaking his
> hand, he continued.) Rise, let us be off to join
> the "Red Head Parshasha" [referring to General
> William Clark at St. Louis].

Due to Petit Corbeau's timely words, at least part of the delegation continued onward. In Washington they met President Martin Van Buren and Secretary of War John C. Calhoun. Little Crow, for one, was greatly impressed with everything he saw. It confirmed in his mind the wisdom and inevitability of Dakota acquiesence to the American government. The trip also produced plans for a great Indian council to be held at Prairie du Chien the following year. Colonal Josiah Snelling reported that the trip had a wonderful effect on the chiefs, that the power, wealth, and numbers of the American people were their constant themes--"many of their stories approach so near the marvelous as to be discredited, such for example is the account of casting a cannon...and the magnitude of our ships."

Source: Lawrence Taliaferro, "Auto-Biography of Maj. Lawrence Taliaferro," *Minnesota Historical Collections* 6 (1894):203-5.

"All our bad thoughts are burned with the ashes of the pipe."

LITTLE CHIEF   August 1825

IN AUGUST 1825 all of the leading Dakota chiefs gathered and accompanied their agent to the great Indian council at Prairie du Chien. The grand congress of Indian nations included delegations from the Chippewa, Sac and Fox, Menominee, Iowa, Winnebago, and Ottawa tribes. General William Clark and Governor Lewis Cass conducted the proceedings, hoping to set well-defined and firmly respected boundaries between all of the tribes of the northwest. The various chiefs were allowed to speak briefly--most expressing their hopes for peace and describing the boundaries of the land they claimed for their tribes. Little, from Lac qui Parle, was the principal Wahpeton Dakota chief. His speech is representative of most speeches made before the commissioners:

> My fathers, I am very much pleased that you are entering on so good a work, and at the advice you have given to our brethren. All our bad thoughts are burned with the ashes of the pipe.
> We come here to speak the truth--we must tell the truth before God [probably the interpreter's translation of a reference to the Great Spirit, or Wakan Tanka] and our fathers....
> I am of the prairie. I claim the land up the River Corbeau to its source, and from there to Otter Tail Lake. I can yet show the marks of my lodges there, and they will remain as long as the world lasts.

Red Wing, who had turned to the Americans before most of his fellow Dakotas after the last war, boasted that although the other chiefs had now thrown their "bad thoughts into the fire," he could not say that any of his had gone there "because, from the good counsel I always got from General Clark and Mr. Boilvin, I had none....I have always been a good man."

Source: *Niles' Register*, Nov. 19, 1825. Little Chief lived till at least 1838, when he complained of Hole-in-the-Day's massacre of three lodges of his Wahpetons. He said that he had met with many misfortunes in his life, but never one "so heavy" as these murders. The chief disappears from the historical record after this. Lawrence Taliaferro Journals, June 23, 1838, MHS.

"...every nation has its customs...."

PINICHON   circa 1820s

PINICHON, OR, HE THAT FEARS NOTHING (Takokipasni), was a Mdewakanton band chief, who inhabited the "Old Village" on the Minnesota River at the mouth of Nine Mile Creek. His father, He Sees Standing Up (Wanyagyainazin), had signed the Pike Treaty of 1805, but died before 1820. During the War of 1812, Pinichon had sided with the British, but as he told agent Taliaferro in 1821, he had "quit these people," and was willing to turn in his British flag, chiefs' medal and gorget. Despite his boast that he had "a strong arm" and would do good in his village, he had the reputation of being a weak leader and an alcoholic. In 1823 his following had become so reduced that the agent told him that "his standing as a chief" would soon cease.

However, the chief had a likeable side as well. William J. Snelling, the son of Colonel Snelling, wrote that, although the chief was "a harmless, worthless, drunken vagabond," he has "a fund of humor that frequently amuses the officers of the garrison and procures him a bottle of whiskey." Once, Pinichon appeared at the fort wearing his worst clothing and having his face blackened with ashes, as was the Dakota custom when in mourning--the chief's brother had just died. Colonel Snelling asked him why he did not array himself in the good black broadcloth of the whites. Pinichon said:

> Father, every nation has its customs; you are
> rich and we are poor. Therefore, we show our
> grief by smearing our faces with soot and you
> attire yourselves in black cloth. But as you do
> not approve of my following the customs of
> my ancestors, to please you I am willing to com-
> promise. Give me a black dress for this occasion,
> and in return, I will give you as much soot as
> shall serve for the purpose of mourning all the
> days of your life!

On another occasion the Colonel asked the chief if the Rum River was so named because rum ran there instead of water. Pinichon replied, "No father, it does not. If it did, I would live on its banks till I had drunk it dry. You would never see me here again."

Sources: William J. Snelling, *Tales of the Northwest* (Minneapolis: University of Minnesota Press, 1936), 222-23; Taliaferro Journal, Sept. 13, 1821. Pinichon died by late 1833 and was succeeded as chief by his son, Good Road.

"In my young days I used to run the buffalo...."

SHAKOPEE   1827

COMPLAINTS ABOUT OLD AGE are universal. Old Shakopee had been a great war chief in his day and had led the largest band of the Mdewakantons. Several months prior to his death, he visited agent Taliaferro at the St. Peter's Agency. He reminisced about the past, and asked for a few presents:

> You see me today. I am like a broken tree-- old and unable to help myself. I hope you will look at me sometimes, and feed the stump.
> In my young days I used to run the buffalo, kill my enemies, and visit your chiefs at a great distance, but now my limbs hang useless, and my body weak.
> My father, I take you by the hand in this my old age. If I am like a woman, treat me not the worse for it.

Source: Taliaferro Journal, Jan. 21, 1828.

"...it is better to die in battle than starve to death...."

BLACK EAGLE and CANE   1829

BLACK EAGLE (WAMDISAPA) was a war chief of the Wahpekute Dakotas, and cousin of the head chief, Cane (Tasagi). After the 1825 peace council at Prairie du Chien, the Wahpekutes had hoped to see some relief from a ravaging war with the Sac and Fox, who had begun to invade Wahpekute hunting grounds (which included much of present day Iowa.) But in late 1828 a Wahpekute hunting camp was attacked by a war party led by the mixed-blood Fox war chief, Morgan. Black Eagle, who had been absent from the village at the time, related the disaster to agent Taliaferro:

> My father, I left my family as I thought in safety and went out to trap a little for myself, but on my return to my lodge everything was destroyed. My wife was killed, her head cut off--her body cut to pieces and thrown into the river like the skin of a slaughtered deer. I felt sore at heart and immediately sent word to my people to join me and revenge my misfortune. But this chief here, my friend [Pinichon], advised us not to go to war until we had seen you and our hunt was over for the winter.
>
> My father, I listened to my friend and you see me here today. My feelings are hard against the Sacs and Foxes, but I am disposed to hear you before I do anything. If you say I am to revenge my wrongs, I will die like a man. My nation, you know, is numerous and can if we all join, drive those dogs who bite us from their lands. We understood, my father, that whenever any of the nations of Red Skins commenced war again that your nation would chastise the aggressors, but this does not appear to be done.

Black Eagle later took it upon himself to avenge his dead by killing the occupants of a single enemy lodge, among the victims a prominent chief who possessed medals and flags. The Dakotas felt obliged to avenge the deaths of relatives, believing that the spirit of the deceased could not go to the country of spirits, or have rest, until the blood of an enemy had been spilled. Cane, whose stepdaughter and child had been taken prisoner by Morgan, told Taliaferro: "We must hunt on our lands or starve. I am going out again and if a cloud [is] over my lands, I must [meet] it, for it is better to die in battle than starve to death, for that is a slow way of dying." As the warfare continued to decimate the small Wahpekute tribe, Cane declared: "We are living on our lands for one hundred years and losing half our people in defending it."

Sources: Taliaferro Journal, April 1, June 17, July 4, 1829, and June 16, 1830.

"This red pipe was given to the red men by the Great Spirit...."

SWIFT MAN   1836

IN 1836 ARTIST GEORGE CATLIN decided to make a trip into the heart of Dakota country to see the famed Pipestone Quarry (in southwestern Minnesota). Arriving at Traverse des Sioux, he was stopped by a party of Dakotas, who were greatly upset about his intentions. They feared that he was an American officer sent by the government to acquire the quarry from the Sioux. Swift Man, the son of a chief, spoke to Catlin of his fears and his realization that one day the whites would own "all" the Dakota lands:

> Brothers, we look at you and we see that you are Chemokemon captains (white men officers). We know that you have been sent by your government to see what that place is worth, and we think the white people want to buy it.
>
> Brothers, we have seen always that when white people see anything in our country, they want to send officers to value it, and then if they can't buy it, they will get it some other way.
>
> Brothers, I speak strong, my heart is strong, and I speak fast. This red pipe was given to the red men by the Great Spirit--it is part of our flesh, and therefore is great medicine.
>
> Brothers, we know that the whites are like a great cloud that rises in the east, and will cover the whole country. We know that they will have all our lands. But if ever they get our Red Pipe Quarry, they will have to pay very dear for it.
>
> Brothers, we know that no white man has ever been to the Pipe Stone Quarry, and our chiefs have often decided in council that no white man shall ever go to it.
>
> Brothers, you have heard what I have to say, and you can go no farther, but you must turn about and go back.
>
> Brothers, you see that the sweat runs from my face, for I am troubled.

Catlin explained that he was not a government officer and risked making the trip anyway. Passing unmolested, he visited the quarry and sent samples of the red stone back east for analysis--it was later named "catlinite" in his honor. The quarry passed from Indian ownership by the Treaty of 1851, although the Sissetons later said that they had not intended that the quarry be included in the land cession.

Source: Michael M. Mooney, *George Catlin Letters and Notes on the North American Indians* (New York: Clarkson N. Potter Inc., 1975), 327.

"I see all your people are well-dressed--we are obliged to wear skins."

BIG THUNDER   **September 23, 1837**

BIG THUNDER (WAKINYANTANKA), also known as Little Crow, succeeded his famous father, Petit Corbeau, as chief by 1834. He became one of the leading spokesmen for the Mdewakanton tribe. In 1837 he was a member of the Dakota delegation to Washington. The chiefs met with Indian Commissioner C. A. Harris, and Secretary of War Joel Poinsett and were encouraged to sell all of their land east of the Mississippi River for one million dollars. Some of the chiefs were reluctant to accept the offer, despite the fact that hard times had come--game was scarce and the price of the traders' goods was high. The son of Shakopee, Standing Cloud, said "we never dreamed of selling our lands until your agent...invited us to come and visit our Great Father." Big Thunder, who had heard in detail of his father's 1824 trip east, apparently recognized the inevitability of the land cession, but he argued for more money:

> My father, some years ago we received an invitation to visit our Great Father. Our friends came here. They told us of your power.
>   My father, since I have been here I have been looking around. I see all your people are well-dressed--we are obliged to wear skins. I am acquainted with your agent at St. Peter's. I have followed your council. I have not arrived to the day when I am to be well off. When the amount is divided among our people it will not be much for each. We have had great difficulty in getting [here]. We have come to see you. We depend upon our Great Father as second to the Great Spirit.

The chiefs requested at least $1,600,000. Poinsett, however, remained firm in his offer, saying that that was the real value of the land, and that the recent land sale of the Chippewas was made at only half of what was offered to the Dakotas. (The government was also in the midst of an economic depression.) Within a few days the chiefs reluctantly accepted the offer--Good Road commented that the whites must "love money."

Sources: Chauncey Bush Minute Book, Bentley Historical Library, Ann Arbor, Michigan; Gary C. Anderson, "The Removal of the Mdewakanton Dakota in 1837: A Case for Jacksonian Paternalism," *South Dakota History*, 10 (Fall 1980):325.

TAMAHA

CHAPTER THREE

PERIOD of INTER--TRIBAL WARFARE, 1837-1850

"They have sprinkled our blood all around."

"...my Great Father should take a stick and bore the ears of these people."

CLOUDMAN   October 5, 1837

WHILE THE DAKOTA DELEGATION was in Washington, they were brought to a meeting with a Sac and Fox group, among them Keokuk and the famous old war chief, Black Hawk. The Dakotas were especially bitter about the warfare between the two tribes, and the fact that Taliaferro had repeatedly restrained them from retaliation. The Mdewakanton chief Cloudman, who in earlier days had been a war chief, said during the council:

> My ears are always open to good counsel, but I think my Great Father should take a stick and bore the ears of these people. They appear to shut their ears when they come into the council.
>
> I always thought myself and my people would be made happy by listening to your advice. But I begin to think the more we listen, the more we are imposed upon by other tribes.
>
> Had I been foolish and given foolish course to my young men, you would not have seen me here today. I might have been at home doing mischief, seeking to revenge what these people have provoked. I have been struck by these men eight times and have lost many of my people....
>
> Grown men like these ought to be men of sense, but I do not believe they have any sense. I cannot place any confidence in them. I have more confidence in that little child (pointing to the son of Keokuk) than in all these large grown men.

The Sac and Fox were just as vehement in their recrimination and sarcasm. Keokuk, responding to Cloudman, said: "Yes, it may be true that our ears are dull and that wood should enter them to make us hear--but the ears of our enemies are stopped, and they must be pierced with iron before they will suffer the voice of our Father to enter."

Sources: Chauncey Bush Minute Book, October 5, 1837; *Niles' National Register*, October 7, 1837.

"....it is the name of a woman...."

WAHPETON CHIEFS and SOLDIERS   Summer 1838

FOR SOME YEARS the Wahpetons of Lac qui Parle had had friendly relations
with two Mississippi Chippewa bands led by two brother chiefs, Strong Ground
and Hole-in-the-Day. However, several of Hole-in-the-Day's relatives were killed
by the Wahpetons in 1837. The chief initially resolved to forget the matter, and
made arrangements to meet and hunt with the Wahpetons in the spring of 1838.
But in the intervening time, Hole-in-the-Day was gripped by feelings of revenge,
and he decided to make the Wahpetons pay dearly. In April 1838 three Wahpeton
lodges cordially received Hole-in-the-Day and a party of his warriors. A feast of
dog meat was made and eaten. Finally, Hole-in-the-Day's dark motive was un-
leashed on the unsuspecting hosts. The massacre of men, women, and children
was swift and brutal. As was common in Indian warfare, the bodies of the victims
were grotesquely cut up and mangled.

The Wahpetons were sore at heart over Hole-in-the-Day's deception and the loss
of their relatives. They were indignant when they received a letter from the
Chippewa chief which said that he would never strike the Sioux another blow,
if the Sioux would not attempt to revenge themselves. The Wahpeton chiefs
and soldiers, Running Walker, Extended Tail Feathers (or Big Curly Head),
Cloudman, Rattling Cloud, Eagle Help, and Warclub that Shows Itself, sent the
following reply:

> **Younger brother of Strong Earth:**
>
> You have written another letter. We have
> seen it. You say that last spring you did some-
> thing bad and that you are sorry about it. Truly,
> how could you not be sorry about it? That action
> wasn't that of a man, but of a woman. This action
> is not the only one for which you should be sorry.
> There are many others as well. Be sorry for all of
> them together. But you still say that we will be
> relatives. Where are the names of the chiefs,
> where are the names of the soldiers? We do not
> see any. Your name is the only one that appears.
> It isn't that of a chief; it isn't that of a soldier;
> but it is the name of a woman. This is why we
> will not say more.

Sources: Edmund C. and Martha C. Bray, ed. *Joseph N. Nicollet on the Plains and Prairies* (St. Paul: Minnesota
Historical Society Press, 1976), 278-79; see also, Mark Diedrich, *The Chiefs Hole-in-the-Day of the Mississippi
Chippewa* (Minneapolis: Coyote Books, 1986), 8. It should be noted that there were two Cloudmans. One was
a Mdewakanton band chief, the second was a Wahpeton soldier, who later became a Wahpeton chief. The Mdewakanton Cloudman died during his imprisonment at Fort Snelling in the winter of 1862-63; the Wahpeton Cloudman
was killed in a fight with the Arickaras in the spring of 1863.

"We can't plant people to grow up as the trees."

RATTLING CLOUD   June 23, 1838

FOLLOWING THE HOLE-IN-THE-DAY MASSACRE, some of the Wahpeton
leaders traveled down to Fort Snelling to report the event. Rattling Cloud, the
principal war chief, addressed Taliaferro, the agent, and Major Joseph Plympton:

> My brother, I address myself to the chief of
> the soldiers--I am a soldier and not a chief. The
> man who struck on us was here last winter to
> visit you. He told me so and that you, my
> brother, advised him to be at peace with us,
> and to throw away the tomahawk--but he did
> not listen. He deceived me and the result of
> my confidence was a great loss to me.
> My father, I am a soldier and I have but
> one word--I speak plain and wish to say a word
> to you this day. The manner in which the
> Chippewas behaved was shameful. They cut up
> our women in a horrid manner. I hope when you
> are prepared, you will satisfy us.
> My father, the steps you take are not
> strong enough. You send words that won't do.
> I put one of my own people under ground for
> doing those people an injury--all know this. We
> wish to get a few of these people into our hands
> for the loss of our friends. We can't plant people
> to grow up as the trees. When they are gone it
> is not in our power to replace them.
> I depend upon you, my father, and my
> brother--I depend on you. If nothing is done
> soon or you can't do it, I rely upon my relations
> here to see us righted. We thought the Hole-in-
> the-Day a good man. He has changed, and here-
> after you never can do anything with him. He is
> lost as a friend to peace.

Source: Taliaferro Journal, June 23, 1838.

"I asked myself if I was a squaw...."

SLEEPY EYES   August 13, 1838

SLEEPY EYES (ISHTABA) was the leader of the Southern Sisseton bands that lived at Swan Lake and Traverse des Sioux. Through the aid of Petit Corbeau, he had become recognized as head chief in 1824 while on the visit to Washington City. Indian Superintendent, T. L. McKenney wrote that the chief was goodnatured and plausible, but lacked distinction as a hunter and warrior. Taliaferro called him an "excellent man" who deserved the attention of white authorities. In later years, missionary Stephen Riggs said that the chief was kind to the whites, though he regretted that Sleepy Eyes was "firmly attached to the religion of his fathers."

In the fall of 1838 the Joseph N. Nicollet expedition, which included the later famous explorer, John Charles Fremont, came across the chief at the Cottonwood River. Sleepy Eyes had a meal with the French cartographer and offered to accompany him west. However, as the chief was suffering from a wound, Nicollet declined the offer. Sometime later, the chief could no longer bear the thought of remaining behind, and soon caught up with them. He explained to Nicollet:

> You have left me sad. I asked myself if
> I was a squaw--I whom the fears of death,
> the wars, and the pains have never stopped.
> You are going to risk dangers. I waited for
> a horse to follow you, not being able to
> walk; the horse did not come in time. I
> mustered my forces. Here I am, I am not
> leaving you.

However, once again Nicollet encouraged the chief to remain at home. Sleepy Eyes resigned himself to this, and came up with an alternative idea: "I give you my son. He is to me the dearest thing on earth, but my heart will be rejoiced if he dies fighting for the whites." The son, indeed, later was killed, but on a Dakota war expedition against the Pottawatomis.

Sources: Bray and Bray, *Nicollet*, 18-19, 116-17; Thomas L. McKenney and James Hall, *The Indian Tribes of North America*, 3 vols. (Edinburgh: J. Grant, 1933), 1:103; Stephen R. Riggs, "Dakota Portraits," *Minnesota History Bulletin*, 2 (1918):494.

"The Great Spirit has given them to us to punish!"

MAZOMANI   July 2, 1839

JUST ONE YEAR had elapsed since Hole-in-the-Day's massacre of the Wahpetons, when the Dakota chiefs met him and his brother, Strong Ground, in council at Fort Snelling. A peace between the two tribes was agreed upon. However, unknown to the Chippewas, two of their number remained behind as the rest proceeded north. These two ambushed and killed the son-in-law of the Mdewakanton chief Cloudman. The Dakotas were infuriated to the uttermost. When war parties had gathered, Mazomani (Walking Iron), the chief of the Little Rapids band of Wahpetons, incited them to action with his address:

> He had consented to allow them to wash the blood of his relatives from their hands and smoked with them the pipe of peace. How has it been repaid? Scarcely has our peace council fire gone out, than they come like the cowardly wolf and spring on the unsuspecting man, and escape with his scalp to grace their wigwams. They escaped because there was none to follow.
>
> But now young men of the Dakotas, you are on their tracks. Let none escape--their women, who expected to dance the scalp dance, and their children, who will grow up and do as their parents have done. Give quarter to none--let them all die.
>
> We have forgiven them time after time; still every peace has been broken by them. Now, we have them in our power. The Great Spirit has given them to us to punish. The blood of our murdered relatives calls loudly for revenge. Let them escape and where will you find them? They do not live as we do in villages on the great rivers, giving an opportunity to any coward to crawl up and kill one of us, as our brave brother was today. They live at home on islands in lakes, and the country is an unbroken forest, where we cannot reach them. They always have had the advantage, and nothing but your courage has so far saved your families. Let us then up and destroy them, since the Great Spirit has delivered them to us!

On July 3 two severe battles took place. One group of Dakotas, under Big Thunder, attacked the unsuspecting Chippewas under Strong Ground on the St. Croix. A second war party led by Red Bird, Bad Hail, Shakopee, and Mazomani surprised Hole-in-the-Day's contingent near the mouth of the Rum River. Over one hundred Chippewas were killed. Young Shakopee (II) made one of his most famous speeches after the battle, pleading with the Dakotas not to leave their wounded behind: "You have poured blood upon me and now you run away and leave me."

Sources: Thomas Hughes, *Indian Chiefs of Southern Minnesota* (Minneapolis: Ross and Haines, Inc., 1969), 38-39; Diedrich, *Chiefs Hole-in-the-Day*, 8-9; Samuel Pond, *The Dakotas or Sioux in Minnesota as they were in 1834* (St. Paul: Minnesota Historical Society Press, 1986), 396. Mazomani was the son of Mazomani I, who died of smallpox on August 21, 1838. Mazomani II was also known as Shade; his brother was Akipa. Mazomani was killed when trying to defect to the whites at the Battle of Wood Lake in 1862.

"...I have brought you the book...."

EAGLE HELP   **1839**

AMONG THE SPIRIT POWERS worshipped by the Dakotas was Takushkanshkan, the spirit of motion or change. Granite boulders were his symbol and sometime dwelling place. The Dakotas ceremoniously painted these stones red, prayed to the spirit (addressing him as Grandfather), and left small offerings. Takushkanshkan was believed to be easily displeased, full of revenge, and the animator of war weapons. The Metamorphose feast was held in his honor.

Eagle Help (Wamdiokiye) was a war shaman among the Lac qui Parle Wahpetons. However, he came under the tutelage of the missionaries, and became the first male Dakota to learn to read and write in his own language. He then assisted the missionaries in their translation of the Bible into the Dakota language. As he became more acquainted with Bible teachings, Eagle Help gradually left off his participation in the traditional Dakota feasts. In 1839 he was sent by the missionaries to Lake Traverse to teach the young men how to read and write. One day he was invited to a sacred feast, but he told them:

> My friends, you make sacred feasts; you worship
> painted stones. Tell me what benefit you or your
> fathers have obtained from these practices? I
> have my father's medicine bag, and I am acquaint-
> ed with all the Dakota customs, but I know of
> no good that comes to us from them. And now
> I have brought you the book [the Bible], by
> means of which we may all become wise; but
> you will still choose to pray to painted stones.

Sources: Mark Diedrich, *The Odyssey of Chief Standing Buffalo and the Northern Sisseton Sioux* (Minneapolis: Coyote Books, 1988), 18; Riggs, "Dakota Portraits," 565; Stephen R. Riggs, *Mary and I: Forty Years with the Sioux* (Boston: Congregational Sunday-School and Publishing Society, 1887), 76-77.

"The Dakotas...make a great wailing over a dead friend."

BLACK EAGLE   1843

BLACK EAGLE, the elderly Wahpekute chief, was no stranger to grief. His wife had been brutally slaughtered by the Sac and Fox in 1828. Members of his band had been killed in other fights. As Black Eagle frequently visited the Sisseton village of Big Walker at Traverse des Sioux, he became acquainted with missionary Stephen R. Riggs and his associates. On July 15, 1843 Riggs's brother-in-law, Thomas Longley, drowned while bathing in the Minnesota River. Black Eagle quietly observed the whites as they buried their relative. A while later, he felt constrained to chide them for not expressing their sorrow in tears and lamentations, saying:

> The ducks and the geese and the deer, when
> one is killed, make an outcry about it, and
> the sorrow passes by. The Dakotas, too, like
> these wild animals, make a great wailing over
> a dead friend--they wail out their sorrow, and
> it becomes lighter; but you keep your sorrow--
> you brood over it, and it becomes heavier.

Riggs remembered the old man's speech, and later wrote: "There was truth in what the old man said. But we did not fail to cast our burden upon the Lord, and to obtain strength from a source which the Black Eagle knew not of." Black Eagle died several years later. What was left of his small band apparently drifted into the following of his son, Inkpaduta (Scarlet Point), who had been outlawed for his involvement in a quarrel which resulted in the killing of Chief Cane in about 1841-42.

Sources: Riggs, *Mary and I*, 104-9; Diedrich, *Famous Chiefs*, 43-47.

"...never has a coward been known among the People of the Spirit Lakes."

SHAKOPEE (II)   August 4, 1843

SHAKOPEE (OR STANDING CLOUD) succeeded his brother, He that Holds Five, as chief of their father's band in the 1830s. To the whites who knew him, he was something of an anomaly. Dr. Thomas Williamson said that although the chief was "a disagreeable man," he had more influence than most of his fellow chiefs. Captain Seth Eastman's wife, Mary, wrote that the chief was "decidedly ugly, but that there was an expression of intelligence about his quick black eye and fine forehead...." The chief was also known for his timidity in warfare, a matter about which even he himself joked. He said once in 1858 that "if the Sioux were all like him, no Chippewas would ever be killed!" Above all, however, Shakopee was known as a great orator. Missionary Samuel Pond said that the chief's speeches "often contained sage counsel and noble sentiments." He was famous for his epigrammatic expressions, such as "No man who was absent from a battle but would have been brave had he been there; no man absent from a council, but would have been wise had he been there."

In 1843 Shakopee was called upon to attend a peace council with the Chippewa chief Hole-in-the-Day and others at Fort Snelling. After gathering his warriors for the trip downriver, Shakopee, an obviously potent politician, told them of his intentions:

> My boys, the Dakotas are all braves; never has a coward been known among the People of the Spirit Lakes [Mdewakantons]. Let the women and children fear their enemies, but we will face our foes and always conquer.
>
> We are going to talk with the white men; our Great Father wishes us to be at peace with our enemies. We have long enough shed the blood of the Chippewas; we have danced round their scalps, and our children have kicked their heads about in the dust. What more do we want? When we are in council, listen to the words of the interpreter as he tells us what our Great Father says, and I will answer him for you; and when we have eaten and smoked the pipe of peace, we will return to our village.

Sources: Mary H. Eastman, *Dahcotah, or Life and Legends of the Sioux Around Fort Snelling* (New York: Arno Press, 1975), 11-12, 110; Samuel Pond Jr., *Two Volunteer Missionaries Among the Dakotas* (Boston and Chicago: Congregational Sunday-School and Publishing Society, 1893), 142-46, 186, 396; Thomas S. Williamson to David Greene, Jan. 28, 1847, American Board of Commissioners for Foreign Missions (ABCFM) Papers, MHS.

"Our bows are good; but we love peace."

SISSETON and WAHPETON CHIEFS   November 14, 1844

FROM THE 1820'S ONWARD, the Northern Sisseton and Wahpeton tribes, and their close allies, the Cut Head Yanktonais, watched with dismay as the Red River Metis conducted annual hunts on the plains of North Dakota, killing thousands of buffalo each year. The Dakotas feared the complete destruction of their commissary. The government failed to outline a boundary between the two parties, and killings resulted. In 1844 a Metis was killed by a Yanktonai. To avenge this loss, the Metis killed eight Sissetons and Cut Heads of Lake Traverse. The leading Sisseton and Wahpeton chiefs, Burning Earth, War Eagle who Cries Walking, Thunder Face, and Running Walker sent a letter of protest to the Metis leader, Cuthbert Grant:

> Friends, we hang down our heads; our wives mourn, and our children cry....The pipe of peace has not been in our council for the last six days.... We are now strangers. The whites [the Metis] are our enemies....The whites have often been in our power, but we always conveyed them on their journey with glad hearts, and something to eat....
>
> Our young men have been killed. They were good warriors; their friends cry. Our hearts are no longer glad. Our faces are not painted....
>
> You owe the Sissetons four loaded carts; they were our relations; the half-breeds are white men: the whites always pay well....The four Yankton[ai]s did not belong to us; but they are dead also....
>
> Tell us if we are to be friends or enemies? Is it to be peace or war? Till now our hands have always been white, and our hearts good.... We are not frightened; we are yet many and strong. Our bows are good; but we love peace: we are fond of our families....Our hearts were not glad when we left you last; our shot pouches were light; our pipes cold; but yet we love peace. Let your answer make our wives happy and our children smile....

In a letter dated December 8, 1844, Grant replied that the Metis had fought only in self defense and that they had "violated no faith," and "broken no peace." He added: "We know you are a brave and generous people; but there are bad people among you." The chiefs eventually decided not to retaliate, although they sent another letter to the Metis with comments from those who had lost friends or family. One Sisseton wrote: "You killed my father...I wish him who made me fatherless, should be my father. He was a chief, a Sisseton warrior, had a gun and a bow, had been scalped young. His feathers reached the ground...."

Sources: Diedrich, *Odyssey of Chief Standing Buffalo*, 11; Alexander Ross, *The Red River Settlement* (Minneapolis: Ross and Haines, Inc., 1957), 325-30.

"I would not do it."

SPIRIT WALKER   1850

MISSIONARIES Thomas Williamson, Stephen Riggs, Gideon and Samuel Pond,
and others labored for years among the Dakotas to convert them to Christ. Although
the results of their work were numerically small, they gained several influential men,
including Little Paul Mazakutemani, John Other Day, Simon Anawangmani, and
Spirit Walker.

Spirit Walker (Wakanmani) was the principal man of a small Wahpeton village at
Lac qui Parle; he was about sixty years old in 1850. He and his relatives regularly
attended services held by Riggs. On one occasion he told the missionary of his
attachment to Christ:

> If anyone should bring me a very fine horse,
> one that could run very swiftly and could
> catch buffalo well, and should say to me,
> "If you forsake the religion of the Bible, I
> will give you this fine horse," I would not do
> it. And if someone should offer me embroid-
> ered leggins and a very fine coat and blanket,
> on condition that I should leave Christ, I
> would not do it. And finally, if someone
> should bring a great deal of what is very good
> to eat, sugar for instance, and should say to
> me, "Throw away this religion and I will
> give you all this," I would not do it.

He also told Riggs that he had been "a great sinner," that he had had ten wives
besides those he had had "secretly," and that he had killed a man in combat
and shared in "the glory and shame of several others." He was presently in a
dilemma over the fact that he had two wives and the missionaries wanted him to
give up one. Spirit Walker had one wife who was willing to be "put away," however
she was the one that he wished to keep! Riggs reported also that the chief was having
to endure persecution for his religious stance--"the Indians are...prophesying that he
will die, and [are] threatening to kill him by their enchantments."

Source: Stephen Riggs to S. B. Treat, May 17, 1850, ABCFM Papers.

"They have sprinkled our blood all around."

BAD HAIL   June 12, 1850

BAD HAIL was a prominent war chief of the Mdewakantons. He early achieved
fame for killing a murderer of the tribe at the request of a tribal council. In 1837
he was a member of the Dakota delegation to Washington. Bad Hail also had close
ties to the Mendota fur trade boss, Henry H. Sibley, due to the fact that Sibley had
a daughter (Helen) by Bad Hail's daughter. By the late 1840s Bad Hail had become
the chief speaker of his tribe. He attracted attention in part because he wore such
a striking costume--a plugged hat, an officers' continental blue coat with red facings,
in addition to his leggings and breechcloth.

In the spring of 1850 the Dakotas killed a number of Chippewas on the Apple
River (in Wisconsin). In retaliation, Young Hole-in-the-Day, son of the Dakota
nemesis--Old Hole-in-the-Day (who died in 1847), killed a Dakota near St. Paul.
Alexander Ramsey, who had become the territorial governor in 1849, and who
lived in St. Paul, was immediately anxious to bring forth peace. The Dakota and
Chippewa chiefs met face to face at Fort Snelling on June 12, 1850. After Ramsey's
address, and a speech by Hole-in-the-Day, Bad Hail gave his talk, as interpreted
by Philander Prescott, the old frontiersman:

> My father, I am going to tell you the truth. I
> hope you will listen to it. I will not go back of
> the treaty [of 1843] . Soon after the treaty was
> signed, the Chippewas came and killed one of
> our braves. Soon after, the Chippewas came down
> and killed three of us, including my sister....Three
> men were killed for whom we claim payment, which
> is not made. That is the reason we struck the Chip-
> pewas this spring....It is very easy for the Chippewas
> to float down the river in their canoes in the night
> and kill us. We have long listened to you and delay-
> ed vengeance....
>
> Old Hole-in-the-Day committed many out-
> rages upon the Sioux in his day, and I am sorry
> to see that his son is walking in his father's foot-
> steps. I hope his counsel will not be listened to.
> The Chippewas came down upon us like wolves
> through the grass. You have called me to shake
> hands with this young man. I have done so
> through respect for you....
>
> I am a soldier, and talk to this young man
> to give him advice. A paper has been laid upon
> your table. I am ashamed of it. I think it must
> have been written by a child. I know all the old
> people around me, both Sioux and Chippewas. I
> have been friendly with them. I have made this
> young man sore, and his father before him. They
> have good reason to know me; but the Chippewas
> came down and struck the last blow; they have
> sprinkled our blood all around. Still, we are willing
> to forget the past.

Source: *Minnesota Pioneer* (St. Paul), June 13, 1850.

42

WABASHA (III)

MARK DIEDRICH
1980

CHAPTER FOUR

THE TREATY PERIOD, 1851-1862

"We have lost confidence in the promises of our Great Father."

"The money comes to us, but will all go to the white men who trade with us."

SLEEPY EYES and BIG CURLY HEAD   July 23, 1851

IN THE HISTORY OF THE EASTERN DAKOTAS, 1851 was a pivotal year. During the summer, treaty commissioners Luke Lea and Alexander Ramsey met with the Upper Dakotas, the Sisseton and Wahpeton, to negotiate a treaty for the sale of all Dakota lands east of Big Stone Lake. After several weeks of delay, Big Curly Head asked for written proposals from the commissioners. The chiefs and headmen counciled about the matter, and finally agreed to take the offer of ten cents per acre, which would produce an annuity of about $68,000 for fifty years. However, according to Dr. Williamson, "The Sioux never offered to sell their lands; but were persuaded and driven to do so, asserting at the time that the price was not an equivalent." This attitude was reflected in Big Curly Head's statement as he signed the treaty:

> Fathers, you think it a great deal you are giving
> for this country. I don't think so; for both our
> lands and all we get for them will at last belong
> to the white men. The money comes to us, but
> will all go to the white men who trade with us.

Sleepy Eyes, too, spoke about his reservations, particularly in regard to the traders:

> You will take this treaty paper home and show
> it to the Great Father, but we want to keep a
> copy here so that we may look at it and see
> whether you have changed it. As to paying our
> debts to the traders, I want to pay them what
> is right, but I would like to know how much I
> owe them. If they have charged me ten dollars
> for a gun, I want them to tell me, and if they
> have charged me ten dollars for a shirt, I want
> them to tell me that.
>   I am a poor man and have difficulty in
> maintaining myself, but these traders wear
> good coats. The prairie country in which I live
> has not much wood. I live along with our traders,
> and they also are poor, but I do not want to pro-
> vide for them. I think it will be very hard upon
> us when the year becomes white, and I would
> like to have some provisions given me for the
> winter. I would also like to have what is mine
> laid on one side; then when we have finished
> business, I will know how many of my relatives
> I can have mercy upon.

However, even as the chiefs spoke of their mistrust and suspicions regarding the treaty and traders' debts which would be paid out of their treaty money, they were unwittingly being led to a signing table to make their marks on the infamous "traders' paper." This paper gave Ramsey the legal ground to make whatever debt payments he deemed fair to the traders, without consulting the Dakotas as to their version of their indebtedness.

Sources: St. Paul *Minnesota Daily Times*, Oct. 24, 1854 (Williamson quote); *Minnesota Pioneer*, July 10 and Aug. 7, 1851 (James Goodhue account of the treaty-making); Hughes, *Indian Chiefs*, 106.

"We will talk of nothing else but that money if it is until next spring."

LITTLE CROW   July 31, 1851

AFTER THE COUNCIL at Traverse des Sioux, treaty negotiations began at Mendota with the Mdewakanton and Wahpekute tribes. Talks immediately stalemated when Wabasha (III) wanted money paid out to the Dakotas due them by the treaty of 1837. Finally, after several days, Little Crow (son of Big Thunder and grandson of old Petit Corbeau), the newest and youngest Mdewakanton chief, felt obliged to speak for his people. A historian wrote: there "ensued another long, constrained and uncomfortable silence, which was finally broken by the deliberate and graceful rising of Little Crow, chief of the Kaposia band, the brainiest, shrewdest, and most influential Indian then west of the Mississippi." Wearing a white shirt with a gaudy neckerchief, a medicine bag suspended about his neck, a red belt with silver buckle, beaded leggings and moccasins, the chief said:

> Fathers, these chiefs and soldiers and others who sit here have something they wish said to you and I am going to speak it for them. There are chiefs who are older than myself, and I would rather they had spoken; but they have put it upon me to speak--although I feel as if my mouth was tied.
>   These chiefs went to Washington long ago and brought back a good report concerning the settlement of our affairs in the treaty made there and they and we were glad. But things that were promised in that treaty have not taken place. This is why these men sit still and say nothing. You perhaps are ashamed of us; but you, fathers, are the cause of its being so.
>   They speak of some money that is due them; it was mentioned the other day to Governor Ramsey, and we spoke about it last fall, but we have not yet seen the money. We desire to have it laid down to us. It is money due on the old treaty, and I think it should be paid; we do not want to talk about a new treaty until it is all paid....We will talk of nothing else but that money if it is until next spring. That lies in the way of a treaty. I speak for others and not for myself.

Due in large part to Little Crow's well-stated demands, the council started forward. After several problems were cleared up, at least as the Indians thought, Little Crow was called upon by the soldiers of the tribe to sign the treaty--there had been rumors that the soldiers would kill the first chief who signed. Undaunted, Crow said:

> Soldiers, it has been said by some of you that the first that signs this treaty you will kill. Now, I am willing to be the first, but I am not afraid that you will kill me. If you do, it will be all right. A man has to die sometime and he cannot die but once. It matters little to me when my time comes, nor do I care much how it comes, although I would rather die fighting my enemies. I believe this treaty will be best for the Dakotas, and I will sign it, even if a dog kills me before I lay down the goose quill.

Source: Return I. Holcombe and Lucius F. Hubbard, *Minnesota in Three Centuries, 1655-1908* (Mankato: Publishing Society of Minnesota, 1908), 2:305-8, 314-16.

"We do not want to be humbugged out of our lands."

LITTLE CROW   May 1852

DUE TO THE TREATY-MAKING of 1851, the Mdewakantons spent little time in their villages, and consequently, the women did not plant their usual gardens. This, along with the scarcity of game, caused many Dakotas to be in a complete state of destitution by spring 1852. They wondered when the treaty would be ratified and when the first money payments would come. A St. Paul newspaper characterized them as "armed paupers," who "lived and hoped on in daily expectation of relief." In the meantime, white settlers were streaming over the Mississippi to occupy Indian land. By mid-May the situation had become intolerable to Little Crow. He assembled his band in St. Paul and made the following speech. It is a rare and remarkable piece of oratory, replete with humorous sarcasm about Governor Ramsey and the treaty negotiations:

> Last year our Great Father made a great fuss about the treaties. He asked us to hitch along and let him sit down on our grounds where we could have a talk together about his buying our land. Our father sat down with us and began to talk with us and whittle a stick and then whistle, and he kept on in that way for almost two moons--kept us waiting there, many bands having come from away up the Missouri River. We got very tired. We danced attendance on our father so long that we raised no corn.
>
> Our father is a devil of an old fellow to hunt, if he can only corner a drove of cattle. Our father is a great glutton; he would go and shoot a cow or an ox every morning, and give us the choice pieces of it, such as the head and the paunch; and there he kept us waiting for six weeks; and when the cattle were nearly all gone, and he had whittled all the sticks he could find, he got up and shut his jackknife, and belched up some wind from his great belly, and poked his treaty at us, saying "I will give you so much for your land."
>
> It is true he said that the Senate at Washington would have to ratify the treaties. Well, we signed the treaties, we could not help ourselves. We went home. We had no corn crops and could find no game to speak of; well, the white settlers came in and showered down their houses all over our country. We did not really know whether this country any longer belonged to us or not. The settlers gave us something to eat, that is certain. They have generally been very kind to us.
>
> But this is what we are waiting to know, whether our father means to take our lands for nothing, or whether he means to pay us the money and the annuities he promised us in the treaties? We do not want to be humbugged out of our lands. We owe debts and we want to pay them. If our father had said, "Move along; you must move along; you shall move along," it is likely we should have had to go; but that was not

LITTLE CROW

the way our father talked to us. He said, "You have no game here, our people are hemming you in, you can have no schools or farming while you live scattered; you owe debts, you need annuities; will you go, my Red Children, if we give you so much?" We thought that was very kind and we said yes. Now what have we? Why, we have neither our lands where our fathers' bones are bleaching, nor have we anything. What shall we do?

Source: *Minnesota Pioneer*, March 18, April 1, May 27, 1852.

47

"...gather us all together on the prairie and surround us with soldiers and shoot us down."

WABASHA and BAD HAIL   July-August 1852

THE TREATY OF 1851 was ratified on June 23, 1852. However, it had been amended to state that the Sioux did not own their reserve--rather, their Great Father would allow them to cultivate the lands for a period of time and then remove them elsewhere. When Wabasha heard the news he commented indignantly:

> There is one thing more which our Great Father
> can do, that is, gather us all together on the
> prairie and surround us with soldiers and shoot
> us down!

In late August the chiefs heard the news formally at Governor Ramsey's house in St. Paul. Bad Hail expressed the mood of the chiefs upon being asked to sign the amended treaty. With Prescott interpreting, he said frankly:

> Father, we fear that our Great Father at Wash-
> ington wishes to drive us to some country to
> starve us to death, and we cannot sign the treaty
> as our Great Father wishes us.

Undeterred, Ramsey hired the influential politician and trader, Henry M. Rice, to give liberal feasts and presents to the chiefs and to convince them to sign the treaty. In about one month Rice accomplished this objective, but only after spending some $25,000 of Indian removal fund money. In early September the chiefs followed Wabasha's lead to make their marks on the treaty papers. Wabasha, however, wanted the Great Father informed that if they were not to have their present reserve, they wanted one on Lake Hokah Mump near the Blue Earth River. But Secretary of the Interior Alex H. Stuart informed the chiefs in a letter of October 2, 1852 that President Millard Fillmore had authorized them a five year occupancy on their Minnesota River reserve "that you may have time to make all necessary preparations to remove to the new country assigned to you...."

Sources: Stephen Riggs to S. B. Treat, July 31, 1852, ABCFM Papers; Donald D. Parker, ed., *The Recollections of Philander Prescott* (Lincoln: University of Nebraska Press, 1966), 185-99; Alex H. Stuart to the Mdewakantons and Wahpekutes, Oct. 2, 1852, Alexander Ramsey Papers, MHS.

"...the traders threw blankets over our faces and darkened our eyes...."

RED IRON   November 22, 1852

RED IRON (MAZASHA, OR COPPER) succeeded Big Walker as chief of the Traverse des Sioux Sissetons in 1846 and signed the Treaty of 1851. In November 1852 he was called to a council with Governor Ramsey and agent Nathaniel McLean, who were accompanied by forty-five Dragoons from Fort Snelling. They wanted Red Iron to sign a receipt to pay off the traders. Red Iron ignored his first summons to the council as Ramsey had refused to allow the warriors to accompany their chiefs, contrary to Dakota custom; when Red Iron did come, Ramsey threatened to break him of his chieftainship. But Red Iron resolutely traded words with the governor:

> When you first sent for us, there were two or three
> chiefs here, and we wanted to wait till the rest would
> come, so that we all might be in council together, so
> we might know what was done, and understand the
> papers we were signing. When we signed the treaty, the
> traders threw blankets over our faces and darkened our
> eyes, and got us to sign papers we did not understand,
> which were not read or explained to us.

Ramsey answered that the Sioux must pay their debts or else he would not pay them their annuities. Red Iron replied sharply:

> Take the money back! If you don't give us the money,
> I will be glad, and all our people will be glad, for we
> will have our land back. That paper was not interpret-
> ed or explained to us. We are told it gives about 300
> boxes [$300,000] of our money to some traders. We
> don't think we owe them so much. We want to pay
> our honest debts, but not the fraudulent ones. Let our
> Great Father send three good men here to examine
> the accounts and tell us how much we owe, and what-
> ever they say we will pay....

Ramsey said that this could not be done, that he was now ready to pay only the annuities. Red Iron held out stubbornly, saying:

> We will receive our annuities, but will sign no papers
> for anything else. The snow is on the ground, and we
> have waited a long time for our money [which] you
> promised us. We are poor and have nothing to eat; you
> have plenty. Your fires are warm, your tepees keep out
> the cold. We have sold our hunting grounds and the
> graves of our fathers. We have sold our own graves. We
> have no place to bury our dead, and yet you will not
> pay us our money for our lands.

Ramsey took Red Iron into custody and placed him under guard until the Sioux changed their minds.

Source: Hughes, *Indian Chiefs*, 96-98. Despite such treatment as this, Red Iron refused to join in the war of 1862. He died in October 1869 at the Lake Traverse Reserve. *St. Paul Daily Press*, Oct. 30, 1869.

"Tonight the blood of the white man shall run like water in the rain."

LEAN BEAR   November 22, 1852

AFTER RED IRON WAS ARRESTED, about 200 Sisseton warriors congregated, among them, Lean (or Poor) Bear, an influential head soldier. Brandishing his scalping knife, and holding his gun in his other hand, he made the following strong appeal:

> Dakotas! The big men [Ramsey and McLean] are here; the Long Knives are here. They have got Maza-sha in a pen, like a wolf. They mean to kill him for not letting the big men cheat us out of our lands and the money our Great Father sent us.
>
> Dakotas! Must we starve like buffaloes in the snow? Shall we let our blood freeze like the little streams? Or shall we make the snow red with the blood of the white braves?
>
> Dakotas! The blood of your fathers talks to you from their graves where we stand. Their spirits come up into your arms and make you strong. I am glad of it! Tonight the blood of the white men shall run like water in the rain, and Mazasha will be with his people.
>
> Dakotas! When the moon goes down behind these hills, be ready and I will lead you against the Long Knives, and the big men who have come to cheat us, and take away our land, and put us in a pen for not helping them to rob our women and children.
>
> Dakotas! Be not afraid. We have many more braves than the Long Knives. When the moon goes down be ready, and I will lead you to their tepees.

However, several influential mixed-bloods intervened, and convinced Lean Bear that it would not be wise to follow through with his plans. Ramsey, fortunately, soon after released Red Iron. However, Ramsey continued to hold back annuities until he could gain the various chiefs' signatures on the Traders' Paper receipt. Red Iron and various Wahpeton chiefs made a written declaration on December 2-3 that they wanted only $130,000 to go for traders' debts and the mixed-bloods. Ramsey ignored this and later turned over $250,000 of the Sisseton-Wahpeton money to attorney Hugh Tyler for distribution (Tyler is thought to have taken a cut of some $50,000 for his role in the money distributions to the treaty claimants--it is believed that Ramsey probably got kickbacks from Tyler.) The American Fur Company took in over $100,000 from the Dakota treaties.

Sources: *Minnesota Democrat* (St. Paul), Jan. 5, 1853; Gary C. Anderson, *Kinsmen of Another Kind* (Lincoln: University of Nebraska Press, 1984), 196-99. Lean Bear became chief of his own Sisseton band by the mid-1850s. He never moved onto the reservation designated by the treaty, but lived apart from the Dakotas in southwestern Minnesota. He was killed by a white settler in August 1862 at Lake Shetek--a man whom he was apparently trying to warn of danger.

"Mr. Sibley offered us seventy horses...."

LITTLE CROW   **Fall 1853**

IN THE AFTERMATH of the Traders' Paper controversy, the government began an investigation of Governor Ramsey's handling of Indian affairs. During the questioning of many chiefs in St. Paul during the fall of 1853, it was established that Ramsey had coerced the Dakotas into signing receipts giving the traders a great deal of money--he did this by refusing to pay the Sioux their annuities until they had signed. Little Crow spoke of other inducements made by the whites:

> **Mr. Sibley, Mr. Alexander Faribault, and many others, asked us to sign the receipt. Mr. Sibley offered us seventy horses, and double-barreled shotguns and pistols to a good many of the band; but we never received them; and Governor Ramsey was present.**

In addition, five Dakotas were being held indefinitely in the guardhouse at Fort Snelling for fighting Chippewas; Ramsey said that he would release them--only if the receipt was signed. Little Crow commented:

> **There was one, my cousin, one the son of the chief Wechonck-pee, or the Star, and one the son of Bad Hail, a first soldier. Governor Ramsey said that their Great Father at Washington told him to retain them in the guardhouse until they [the chiefs] signed the paper; and to retain their money and not pay it to them until they signed it. If it had not been for these things we would not have signed the paper all the winter.**

Star, the chief of the Cloudman band, added that the Dakotas were kept waiting for two months, and no provisions were issued to them by the agent: "They wanted us to die of hunger." The investigators concluded in their report that Ramsey was guilty of fraud in three areas: 1) he received treaty money in gold and changed it to paper currency, apparently making a profit by the conversion; 2) he and his secretary, Hugh Tyler, took a fee of ten to fifteen per cent for acting as attorneys for claimants of treaty money; and 3) Ramsey refused to let the Dakotas distribute their own money. However, the Senate exonerated him.

Sources: 33rd Congress, 1 session, *Senate Executive Document*, no. 61, 1853-54 (serial 699), pp. 59, 172-73; Gary C. Anderson, *Little Crow, Spokesman for the Sioux* (St. Paul: Minnesota Historical Society Press, 1986), 209; Anderson, *Kinsmen of Another Kind*, 194-99.

"We...wish to live and die where our Great Father has given the land to us forever."

LITTLE CROW   February 15, 1856

DUE TO THE TRADERS' PAPER SCANDAL associated with the Treaty of 1851, many of the Dakotas retained ill feelings towards the government-licensed traders. The controversies continued after the Dakotas were removed to their reservation on the upper Minnesota River, as the various trading outfits set up shops near the agencies. The prominent traders were Nathan and Andrew Myrick, Joseph Brown, Louis Robert, and William Forbes. During the winter of 1855-56, some of these men circulated a paper to gain Dakota signatures on statements that the tribe wanted to remove from their present reserve to other lands and have their annuities paid off; furthermore, it said that the Dakotas admitted to being greatly in debt to the trading posts and that they wanted to pay the traders off. Apparently, Wabasha was given $2,000 to sign the paper.

Little Crow, Shakopee, and a few other headmen were mortified by the matter, and went to agent Richard G. Murphy at the Redwood Agency. Little Crow made the following speech which he wanted recorded as a letter to the Great Father:

> We say the Mdewakanton bands do not owe these traders anything, for we paid all our traders in 1851 and have not asked them for anything since. If any of our young men or women have bought ribbons of the traders, they must individually pay out of their own money when it is given to them by our Great Father at the annual payments; and if it is just, they will do so.
>
> We see a great deal of work done on our own land, and hope every year to see more so that we may soon be able to live as our Great Father has told us we must do--by digging the ground and taking care of cattle. We have already a large field for each of our villages, and our Great Father [can] see many small farms with fences and houses like the Americans. We have a mill to make us boards for our houses, and are soon to have a mill to grind our corn. We will not throw these things away to go to any other place, but wish to live and die where our Great Father has given the land to us forever. Our annuity is small but we are always glad to have it, and so will our children and grandchildren to the end of the fifty years. So we say we will not take their money now or shorten the time for which the annuity is to be paid us.
>
> Now we know very well that when the white men ask us to sign a bad paper, they are always afraid to talk to us before our father, the agent, and we are sure this paper that they ask us to sign now must be a very bad one or they would not give a chief $2,000 to put his name to it. We therefore ask our Great Father not to look at any such paper unless it is sent to him by the agent our Great Father has sent here to advise us and take care of our property and read over to us by his interpreter.

Source: Petition of Chetanwakuamani and others, Feb. 15, 1856, Office of Indian Affairs, St. Peter's Agency, Letters Received, roll 762. Little Crow frequently used his grandfather's personal name, Chetanwakuamani, or Hawk that Hunts Walking.

"...the taking of their guns would mean the burial of their babes...."

INKPADUTA   February 1857

INKPADUTA (SCARLET POINT), the son of Black Eagle, had lived apart from
most of the eastern Dakotas after being banished for his role in the death of the
Wahpekute chief Cane in about 1842. With a small group of followers, he lived
by hunting and fishing, and some planting, on the upper Des Moines River and westward in northern Iowa. During the bitter cold winter of early 1857 he and his men
were hunting a herd of elk near Smithland. During the chase, one of the Indians
killed a white man's dog after it had bitten him; the white man severely beat the Indian.
Later, a posse of white settlers surrounded Inkpaduta's camp of about ten lodges on
the Little Sioux River. They demanded that the Indians turn over all the guns they
possessed. Inkpaduta, with Half-Breed Charley as his interpreter, remonstrated in
a speech of which only the substance has survived:

> He declaimed against such unwarranted proceedings
> by his white neighbors. His people or himself had
> done no wrong to the white folks. He was taken by
> surprise, a surprise at the faithless and heartless re-
> quest that came from people who boast of magnanimity
> and pride themselves in their justice to the cruelly
> wronged. With the deep snow--the cold winter--an ice
> bound plain, shortage of provisions in the camp, the
> taking of their guns would mean the burial of their
> babes--their wives, and even the men themselves, in
> the falling snow.

Captain Seth Smith, who headed the posse, told Inkpaduta to "go to the Omahas,"
who lived to the south at Council Bluffs. The chief replied: "To go to the Omahas
unarmed would be going to a speedier death, but nonetheless a surer one." The
Dakotas had no choice but to give up their guns; the whites tore down the lodges
and departed. Inkpaduta and his band of some thirty people began a northerly
march. After a further dispute with white settlers of Peterson, Inkpaduta and his
men grew angry and sullen. They commenced a massacre of some forty white
settlers near Spirit Lake. History books have branded Inkpaduta the greatest of
the Dakota outlaws, but what of the provocation of the Smithland posse?

Sources: Joseph H. Taylor, "Inkpaduta and Sons," *North Dakota Historical Quarterly*, 4 (Oct. 1929-July 1930):
158; Diedrich, *Famous Chiefs*, 42-57; *Henderson Democrat*, May 7, 1857--report by Joe Coursalle.

"Indians had dark skin, but yet had five fingers and two eyes...."

LITTLE PAUL   June 1857

LITTLE PAUL MAZAKUTEMANI (Shooting Iron Walking) was the leading orator of the Wahpeton tribe through the late 1850s and early 1860s. He was converted to Christianity by the missionaries, and was elected president of Stephen Riggs's Hazelwood Republic, composed of various Dakotas who had set aside Indian dress, cut their hair, and taken up farming near Yellow Medicine Agency.

In the spring of 1857 Little Paul, John Other Day, and Iron Hawk risked their lives to ransom captive Abbie Gardner from Inkpaduta's band. Agent Charles Flandrau brought the girl and her rescuers to St. Paul in June, where Little Paul addressed territorial governor Samuel Medary:

> The American people are a great people--a strong nation; and if they wished to, could kill all our people, but they had better judgement, and permitted the Indians to go themselves, and hunt up the poor girl who was with bad Indians. We believed when we left our kindred and friends that we would be killed ourselves; but notwithstanding this, we desired to show our love to the white people. Our father could have sent troops after Inkpaduta's band but that would have created trouble, and many innocent people would have been killed. That is the reason we desired to go ourselves....
>
> The Wahpetons and Sissetons made a treaty with the whites, but we are fearful even they will get into trouble [like Inkpaduta who had not signed the treaty.] There are good and bad men everywhere--could not point to any nation where all were good. Among the Chippewas, the Sioux of the Missouri, and the Red River half-breeds, there were good and bad men.
>
> The Wahpetons and Sissetons had sold their lands to their Great Father; he had pity on them and gave them a reserve here to live upon; but they were not always well treated. Indians had dark skin, but yet had five fingers and two eyes, and therefore wanted to be as much respected as the whites.
>
> We want to become as industrious, and as able to do something for ourselves, as the whites are. We have a church, and I attend it every Sunday, and hear good advice. We want good counsel; there were bad Indians but we desired to behave well. We want this known and considered by our Great Father at Washington. The whites told us to stop making war and lay down the tomahawk. The advice was good, and we have followed it, and now our women can plant in peace.

A few days later, Governor Medary gave Flandrau $1200 to divide among the three Dakotas for their services--however, he could do nothing about the white racism which was stirred up by the Inkpaduta troubles.

Source: *St. Paul Pioneer and Democrat*, June 24, 1857.

"A man of another band has done wrong and we are to suffer for it."

LITTLE PAUL   August 10, 1857

IN THE WAKE OF THE SPIRIT LAKE MASSACRE, the government adopted a policy of forcing the Dakotas to punish their own people, instead of relying on its own military might. This seemed incomprehensible to the Dakotas and for a time they resisted. Government officers then threatened to withhold annuities until the Dakotas complied. Eventually, in order to avert a war, Little Crow, White Lodge, Running Walker, and A. J. Campbell headed an expedition against Inkpaduta. They killed several of Inkpaduta's men, but Inkpaduta escaped to the Yanktonais on the James River. On August 10 Superintendent William J. Cullen told the Sioux that they must go out again. Little Paul spoke out:

> The soldiers have appointed me to speak for them. The man who killed the white people did not belong to us, and we did not expect to be called to account for the people of another band. We have always tried to do as our Great Father tells us. One of our young men brought in a captive woman. I went out and brought the other. The soldiers came up here [Yellow Medicine] , and our young men assisted to kill one of Inkpaduta's sons at this place. Then you spoke about our soldiers going after the rest. White Lodge said he would go, and the rest of us followed....The soldiers here say that they were told by you that a thousand dollars would be paid for killing each of the murderers. Their Great Father does not expect [us] to do these things without money....We wish the men who went out paid for what they have done.
>
> I am not a chief among the Indians. The white people have declared me a chief, and I suppose I am able to do something. We have nothing to eat, and our families are hungry. If we go out again we must have some money before we go. This is what the soldiers have wished me to say....
>
> All of us want our money now very much. We have never seen our Great Father, but have heard a great deal from him, and have always tried to do as he has told us. A man of another band has done wrong, and we are to suffer for it. Our old women and children are hungry for this. I have seen ten thousand dollars sent to pay for our going out. I wish the soldiers were paid for it. I suppose our Great Father has more money than this.

The Indian Department eventually backed down and made the annuity payment, but apparently no special payment was made to those 100 or so Dakotas who served the government in going against Inkpaduta. In 1858 Little Crow brought the matter of payment up again and received a gun and various other provisions.

Source: Council of Sissetons and Wahpetons, August 10, 1857, OIA, St. Peter's Agency, L.R.

"They will find old Shakopee lying on his belly holding on to his country with his teeth...."

SHAKOPEE (II)   circa Summer 1857

THE INKPADUTA OUTBREAK brought out much prejudicial talk by the whites against the Dakotas. Agent Flandrau reported that the "excitement" has been laid "to the door of the entire Sioux nation." There was a call for driving the Dakotas out of the territory. Shakopee was aware of the anti-Indian sentiment, and told Flandrau:

> **Tell the Great Father that Shakopee will
> never leave his country voluntarily, that
> when he sends his soldiers to take him away,
> they will find old Shakopee lying on his belly
> holding on to his country with his teeth, toes,
> fingernails and eyelids, and they will have to
> tear him away.**

Flandrau then watched the chief enact out his words. He commented years later: "Although I knew there was a good deal of gasconade about the old fellow, I could not help feeling that had I been in his place, I would have been inclined to die on the field rather than have surrendered the heritage which contained the bones of my ancestors."

Sources: Stephen Riggs to S. B. Treat, August 13, 1857, ABCFM Papers; *St. Paul Pioneer and Democrat*, June 24, 1857; Charles E. Flandrau, *Recollections of the Past in Minnesota* (St. Paul: Pioneer Press, 1881), 6 (from a lecture given on Feb. 4, 1881). Shakopee died in the summer of 1862, and it was said that if he had lived longer he might have prevented the outbreak of war, for as Big Eagle said, "he was for the white men and had great influence." Return I. Holcombe, ed., "A Sioux Story of the War: Chief Big Eagle's Story of the Sioux Outbreak of 1862," *Minnesota Historical Collections*, 6 (1894):386.

"Drive us not away, we entreat, we implore, we beseech, we supplicate."

SISSETON and WAHPETON HEADMEN   circa January 1858

THE INSISTENT CRY for the removal of all the Dakotas from Minnesota Territory caused the Upper Dakota chiefs and headmen to react with a petition which was partially published in several newspapers. It was written up by Stephen Riggs. In substance, the Dakotas asked for the removal of all the whites from the west side of the Mississippi. They asked this because they felt that the Treaty of 1851 had not been fulfilled--houses, mills, fields, and other things had not been provided for them. Furthermore, they had been unjustly charged of complicity in the Inkpaduta outbreak. They had also heard that the Great Father wanted them to move farther still from "the graves of their forefathers." Exhibiting a profound naivete, they said that they wanted Congress to restore them again "to the inheritance" of their fathers. In closing, they stated:

> Finally, if our memorial, to have the white people all removed from our borders to the east side of the Mississippi cannot be granted, at least grant us the privilege of living in peace in the land we now inhabit, and which has been guaranteed to us by the most solemn compact. Enjoin it upon our white neighbors to live in friendship with the poor red man whose country they occupy. Help us to become civilized and educated here. Drive us not away, we entreat, we implore, we beseech, we supplicate.

Source: *St. Cloud Visiter*, February 18, 1858.

"...after a while I will have nothing left."

LITTLE CROW   **May 28, 1858**

IN LATE FEBRUARY 1858, Little Crow and many Dakota chiefs and headmen were brought to Washington by the new Dakota agent, Joseph R. Brown. They had hoped to have the Indian Department rectify the unfulfilled promises of past treaties. They were shocked when the Indian Commissioner, Charles E. Mix, wanted them to make another treaty by which they would cede half of their present reservation. Little Crow, in particular, was angered and disillusioned, because he had been to Washington in 1854 to help secure a presidential promise that the Sioux would own their reserve forever. With Antoine J. Campbell interpreting, Crow fired back:

> That is the way you all do. You use very good language, but we never receive half what is promised or which we ought to get. I came here about the reserve in 1854; I recollect you [pointing to the recorder] very distinctly; and you were then writing at the table as you are now, surrounded by papers. You then promised us that we should have this same land forever; and yet, notwithstanding this, you now want to take half of it away. We ought, when we meet to do business, talk like men and not like children....
>
> When we came here, I thought we would do business...but it appears you are getting papers all around me, so that, after a while, I will have nothing left. I am going to see that [treaty] paper which you gave the agent, and if, after examining it, I shall find anything good in it, I will come and see you again; and when I do, you will hear me talk like a man, and not like a child!

A few days later Little Crow and the delegation returned to the Indian Office. The chief was extremely upset to learn that the Sioux did not have permanent ownership of their land after all. President Franklin Pierce had failed to issue an executive decree to that effect. Little Crow complained bitterly: "You gave us a paper...and we had it explained, and from that it would seem that the Sioux Indians own nothing! When I saw that paper it made me ashamed. We had, we supposed, made a complete treaty, and we were promised a great many things, horses, cattle, flour, plows, and farming utensils, but it now appears that wind blows it off."

But Little Crow's remonstrations were in vain. All that was left for him to do was to try and obtain the best deal possible. Unfortunately, the Dakotas took the government officials at their word, that the Sioux would receive $1.25 per acre for the new land cession--the Senate later reduced this to thirty cents, and traders' claims took almost the entire sum!

Source: Lower Sioux Indians in the Indian Office, May 28, June 4, 1858, in Documents Relating to the Negotiations of Ratified and Unratified Treaties...1801-1869, OIA, microfilm T494, roll 6, National Archives Record Group 75.

"We have lost confidence in the promises of our Great Father...."

LITTLE CROW   June 1858

WHILE THE TREATY NEGOTIATIONS dragged on, the Dakota chiefs visited their old agent, Lawrence Taliaferro. Little Crow had been greatly disheartened by the government's attempts to coerce his people into signing away half of their reservation and to live "like white people"--that is, to cut their hair, wear white man's clothing, and take up farming. The Dakotas had particularly lost faith in their agents, although they still refused to believe that the Great Father would ever do them wrong. In Taliaferro's time, the Indians viewed the agent as a friend, who would protect and guide them. However, after Taliaferro left, it seemed to the Dakotas that agents such as Amos Bruce, Nathaniel McLean, Richard Murphy, and particularly Joseph Brown, no longer had the tribe's interests at heart, but rather were willing to collaborate with "the traders" in defrauding the Dakotas of what the Great Father had given them. With A. J. Campbell (the son of Taliaferro's long time interpreter, Scott Campbell) interpreting, Little Crow despairingly recounted their recent history with the government:

> My old father, we have called upon you; we love you; we respect you; we are here none but children; our old chiefs are all gone; we don't know what to do; they want us to divide our lands and live like white people. Since you left us a dark cloud has hung over our nation. We have lost confidence in the promises of our Great Father, and his people; bad men have nearly destroyed us.
>
> You took my grandfather with you to this great city in 1824; you took my father also to this city in 1837; he [Big Thunder] did good for our people; he made a good treaty, because you stood by him; he told me so, and that I must always mind your talk for it was good and true. "No sugar in your mouth"; the nation had no better friend. My grandfather [Petit Corbeau] repeated the same words to us--in my ears. I loved you from my youth, and my nation will never forget you. If ever we act foolish and do wrong, it is because you are not with us.
>
> How is it? You counseled our nation for more than twenty-one years, and since you left we have had five agents as our fathers; a man took your place, A. I. Bruce, he was a fool, and had to leave soon; then came another, and so on. We failed to get a friend in any one like you; they all joined the traders. We know your heart, it feels for your old children.

Wabasha added that Little Crow had spoken the mind of all present; he said that he found it hard to believe that Joseph Brown could be their agent--"We are Indians, but we have no confidence in Mr. Brown." Brown was married to a mixed-blood Dakota woman, but had gained an ill reputation among the Dakotas from his long years in the trade.

Source: Taliaferro, "Auto-Biography," 253-54. Dr. Williamson reported that many Dakotas "disliked and distrusted Brown before he was appointed agent, and have looked on all his conduct in the most unfavorable light." See, Diedrich, *Odyssey of Chief Standing Buffalo*, 30, 33, 36, and Diedrich, *Famous Chiefs*, 69-70.

"We want to pay all we justly owe."

LiTTLE CROW   December 3, 1860

THE LOWER DAKOTA CHIEFS and headmen were called away from their winter
hunts to meet with Superintendent William J. Cullen on December 1, 1860 at the
Episcopal mission schoolhouse at the Lower Agency. Although three important
chiefs--Wabasha, Wakute, and White Dog--were absent, Cullen broke the news that
the Senate would pay the Dakotas only thirty cents per acre for the land cession
made in 1858. When he asked them how they would pay their traders' debts, Little
Crow replied that they would have to consult with their people.

Afterwards, various traders, including agent Joseph R. Brown, Henry Sibley (the
governor), Nathan Myrick, and Jerome Fuller, spoke with the chiefs. Some of the
Dakotas said that they opposed paying the traders, and the traders quickly threatened
to shut down their stores. Little Crow then said that they should pay what they justly
owe, and the others finally said that Crow was right. They met again with Cullen on
December 3; Little Crow made the following speech, with A. J. Campbell interpreting:

> We have talked among ourselves and with our young
> men and I have been asked to say that we wish to
> have our debts paid up to the present time. By the
> treaty at Washington we set apart seventy thousand
> dollars to pay our debts, and to purchase articles to
> bring home, but as we did not bring anything home
> with us, we wish our debts to be paid out of the
> seventy thousand dollars, and if that is not sufficient
> to pay all our debts we want enough taken from the
> balance of our money we are to receive for the land
> on the other side of the river to pay up all we owe.
> 　　We want our debts paid. We do not want to
> have the traders running after us hereafter when-
> ever we kill a muskrat or mink to get the skin on our
> credits.
> 　　...Father, we want you and our Great Father
> at Washington to examine the traders' books and
> see how much is due to each and have the amount
> paid. We want to pay all we justly owe.

Unfortunately, by February 13, 1861, Cullen had decided to approve claims against
the Lower Dakotas to the amount of $102,000. The problem was that the low price
given for the land sale only gave them a payment of $96,000. Later that summer the
chiefs were frantic when they learned that all of their treaty money was going to be
paid to the traders without ever having reached their own hands first. In October,
Little Crow headed a full delegation of chiefs and told the new agent that they had
never agreed to pay the claims against their money unless it was sent to them, and
the claims were submitted to them in open council: "Tell our Great Father that it
is hard for him to expect our hearts to be good when he permits men with bad hearts
to do us wrong so often."

Sources: Statements of Councils, William J. Cullen, April 8, 1861, St. Peter's Agency, special case 288, C1020-
1861, National Archives, record group 75; Henry B. Whipple to Ezekiel G. Gear, Nov. 5, 1862, Letterbooks, Whipple Papers; Nathan Myrick testimony, 1886, Sioux Claims, Special Files, no. 274, and Thomas J. Galbraith to Clark
W. Thompson, Oct. 21, 1861, Special Files, no. 228, microfilm in MHS. Bishop Whipple later claimed that Little
Crow ended up with a new wagon the next day after the council, implying that the chief might have been bribed.
However, Wabasha later said that the chiefs present received horses, guns, and blankets--indicating a general dis-
tribution--not a particular "bribe" of one chief.

RED OWL   June 25, 1861

THE SOLDIERS' LODGE was a Dakota organization of men which took responsibility for policing communal hunts. However, by the late 1850s, some 150 Lower Dakotas formed their Lodge in order to have a stronger voice in tribal politics. Their speaker was Red Owl, the head soldier of Wabasha's band. Bishop Whipple commented about his oratory: "When Red Owl spoke, his words seemed to sway his hearers as leaves are moved by the wind."

On June 25, 1861 Red Owl spoke in council with the new Dakota agent, Thomas J. Galbraith, who had replaced the much-disliked Joseph Brown. Galbraith declared that he had come only to look after the interests of his red children. Actually, he was only in office as a result of a conspiracy hatched by Minnesota congressmen to obtain jobs for political friends, and in numerous ways defraud the Dakotas of their money. Red Owl expressed skepticism about Galbraith's intentions, as well as his tribe's disillusionment with the government over the late treaty, and the questionable conduct of agent Brown. Unfortunately, only the substance of the speech was recorded by a Minneapolis newspaper reporter as it was translated by Philander Prescott:

> They had been promised all these things before, and had been cheated out of them. The property that had been promised and...sent them by the government, had somehow not reached them. They gave their lands to the Great Father at Washington... but the money has been stolen or lost, somehow, and they had not had more than enough to cover the nakedness of the women and children. While the whites, and especially the Great Father...had full, round faces...and had fine clothes, his tribe was ragged, and he himself was now so hungry that he was scarcely able to stand up to represent his people. Five thousand dollars worth of goods were paid for with their money, and yet had been taken by the late agent to a distant part of the country...for storage, and much had not been returned....They wanted a storehouse of their own where the goods cannot slip through anybody's fingers! Red Owl complained loudly of their former agent, Brown [who had] hardly been there at all this year, but would sometimes come at night and go away before daylight....Red Owl also complained that the large sum appropriated for the education fund...had all been used up in building the score of worthless houses in the vicinity.

Galbraith ignored the speech apparently, and broached the subject of the Dakotas allowing white settlers to lay claim to reservation land if they paid $1.25 per acre. Red Owl replied: "The Great Father has plenty of land elsewhere which he can give to these white children of his who are settled on our lands which the Great Father gave us."

Sources: *Minneapolis State Atlas*, July 3, 1861; Galbraith to Clark W. Thompson, July 24, 1861, St. Peter's Agency, LR, roll 763. Red Owl soon after converted to Christianity, took ill and died suddenly on August 23, 1861. *St. Paul Pioneer and Democrat*, Sept. 3, 1861.

"Red man has no Great Spirit book."

WABASHA   **1862**

BY 1862, NEEDLESS TO SAY, the Dakotas were thoroughly disheartened and dejected over the outcome of the Treaty of 1858. In addition, they were bitter about the traders, who had received all the money from the late treaty, and now had the gall to withhold credits from the many Indians who still made a living from hunting. To make matters worse, the missionaries, although sympathetic to the Dakotas' plight, wanted to see them abandon their traditional religion and culture. Bishop Henry Whipple visited the Lower Agency at Redwood and was appalled at witnessing a scalp dance near the Episcopal missionhouse--especially because he had known the Chippewa who was killed. He told Wabasha that the Great Spirit saw the Sioux laughing over their bloody hands and that He was angry: "Some day He will look Wabasha in the face and ask him, 'Where is your Ojibway brother?' " Wabasha replied:

> **White man goes to war with his own brother who lives in the same country [referring to the Civil War], and kills more [people] than Wabasha can count as long as he lives. Great Spirit looks down from heaven and says, "Good white man. Has my book. Me love him very much. I have a good place for him when he dies. Red man has no Great Spirit book. Poor man. He goes, kills one Indian, only ONE man (holding up his little finger.) Great Spirit very mad--put Red man in bad place." Wabasha don't believe it.**

Source: George C. Tanner, *Fifty Years of Church Work in the Diocese of Minnesota* (St. Paul: Published by the Committee, 1909), 389. Whipple wrote later that old Wabasha, "one of nature's noblemen," had become a Christian.

"They have seen the red man's face turned towards the setting sun...."

WABASHA   July 5, 1862

BISHOP HENRY B. WHIPPLE visited the Lower Agency at Redwood in early July 1862. He witnessed the laying of the cornerstone for the new Protestant Episcopal "Church of St. John." The following day, on July 5, he went to visit Wabasha, the principal chief of the Mdewakanton Dakota. Wabasha had been waiting to hear if a law could be passed by Congress so that the Indians might secure their homes by a patent. The Bishop said that this had been accomplished, but went on to speak of his frustration concerning the opposition of the medicine men to the mission, and their dances held on the Sabbath. Wabasha's reply was "a beautiful speech," wrote Whipple, "expressed with much grace":

> Your words have made my heart very glad. You have spoken to me as a father speaks to the child whom he loves well. You have often come to see us, and you know the Indians are not like their white brothers. They have not your ways nor have you our ways.
>
> Our Great Father at Washington bought our homes and promised to help us to become like our white brothers. He said to us, when in Washington, go home and try to live like your white brothers, and in five years we will help you more than we have ever done.
>
> Four winters have passed and the fifth is nigh at hand. We think our Great Father may have forgotten his red children and our hearts are very heavy. The agents he sends to us seem to forget their father's words before they reach here, for we often think they disobey what he has said.
>
> You have said you were sorry to see my young men engaged still in foolish dances. I am sorry. I wish they would be like white men. Sometimes I think they have these old customs hang around them like a garment of their wild life...because their hearts are sick. They don't know whether these lands are to be their home or not. They have seen the red man's face turned towards the setting sun, and feel afraid that many more long journeys are [coming] for themselves and children. This makes them uneasy and they never try to be different. If the Great Council at Washington would do as they promised, then my people would see they meant what they said. The good Indian would be like the white man, and the bad Indian would seek another home.
>
> I have heard of your wise words to our Great Father and that he will now give the Indians who live like white men deeds for their land, and my heart is glad. You have none of my blood in your veins, but you have been always a true friend to the Dacotah. I will repeat your words to the wise men of our people. Often when I sit alone in my tepee they will come back to me and be like sweet music in my heart.

Whipple later felt that Wabasha's words were "a forerunning sign of the coming awful massacre."

Sources: Henry B. Whipple Diary, July 5, 1862, Protestant Episcopal Church Papers, MHS; Henry B. Whipple, "The Cause of Indian Wars," ca. 1868, Whipple Papers; Henry B. Whipple, "The Civilization and Christianization of the Ojibway," *Minnesota Historical Collections* 9 (1901):132.

TAOPI (WOUNDED MAN)

CHAPTER FIVE

WAR IN MINNESOTA, AUGUST—SEPTEMBER 1862

"When men are hungry they help themselves."

"When men are hungry they help themselves."

LITTLE CROW   circa August 7, 1862

DUE TO POOR HUNTS in the winter of 1861-62, as well as crop failure the
year before, and the fact that many traders had begun to restrict giving out provisions to the Sioux on credit, many of the Dakotas, particularly the hunters and
their families,were very destitute. They eagerly expected their annuities for 1862,
although rumors began in the spring that only half of it would be paid to them, as
the other half had supposedly been disbursed to trader claimants in Washington.
Still, superintendent of Indian affairs Clark W. Thompson came back from Washington in early June and set payment dates for the Sioux in early July. Evidence
indicates that he and agent Galbraith brought up annuity money in treasury notes
or "greenbacks," rather than the customary gold coin. On broaching the subject
to the Indians, there was immediate outrage as greenbacks were valued at anywhere
from thirty to fifty per cent of gold; the superintendent immediately called off the
payment and went back to St. Paul to wire the Indian Office for gold specie.

In the meantime, thousands of Upper Dakotas at Yellow Medicine were in a state
of near-starvation, and Galbraith refused to issue them provisions until the annuity
money came. On August 4 the Dakotas broke into the warehouse, and Galbraith
was forced to issue goods in order to avert a possible massacre. By August 6 Captain
John S. Marsh arrived from Fort Ridgely and ordered Galbraith to issue all of
the Upper Sioux their provisions. Little Crow then asked the agent to issue goods
to the Lower Dakotas as well, because many were likewise in a starving condition.
His words were interpreted by John P. Williamson, son of the old missionary:

> We have waited a long time. The money is ours,
> but we cannot get it. We have no food, but here
> are these stores, filled with food. We ask that you,
> the agent, make some arrangement by which we
> can get food from the stores, or else we may take
> our own way to keep ourselves from starving. When
> men are hungry they help themselves.

Although the traders, particularly Andrew Myrick, declared that the Sioux could
"eat grass," the agent finally promised to issue goods at the Lower Agency. However, Galbraith, feeling that the Indian Department was trying to oust him from
office, and secretly carrying the guilt of having embezzled Sioux money, was determined to resign: he had taken up the notion that he would raise a company of volunteers for the Union Army and lead them as their officer. Arriving at the Lower
Agency on August 13 with a number of recruits, he continued his recruiting activi-
ties until leaving for Fort Ridgely on Friday, August 15. He made the inestimable
error of not issuing goods as he had promised. Mrs. Sarah Wakefield later wrote
that the Lower Dakotas "were very angry because the agent did not stop and have
a council with them and give them goods and provisions like the upper Indians."
Furthermore, she reported that the traders told the Dakotas that they would not
receive their money, that "the agent was going away to fight and they would have
to eat grass like cattle...." Nobody as yet knew that Secretary of the Treasury
Salmon P. Chase had finally given orders to issue the annuity money in gold,
and that it left New York on August 11; it was to arrive at Fort Ridgely on August
18--one day too late to prevent the Dakota War.

Sources: On the annuity money problems, see Riggs, *Mary and I*, 171-73, Galbraith to Whipple, May 31, 1862
and Hinman to Whipple, June 19, 1862, Whipple Papers, and Oscar G. Wall, *Recollections of the Sioux Massacre*
(Lake City, MN: Home Printery, 1908), 19; Crow's speech, in Winifred W. Barton, *John P. Williamson: A Brother
to the Sioux* (New York: Fleming H. Revell, 1919), 48-50; Sarah F. Wakefield, *Six Weeks in the Sioux Tepees*
(Shakopee, MN: Argus Book and Job Printing Office, 1864), 10-11.

"Taoyateduta is not a coward!"

LITTLE CROW   **August 18, 1862**

ON SUNDAY, AUGUST 17, 1862, a fateful day for the eastern Dakotas, several young men of Shakopee's band (living at Rice Creek) killed a number of white men and women at Acton. They arrived at their village late that night, and a council was held. Little Six, the son of Shakopee, suggested that they consult Little Crow.

Little Crow's village was several miles southeast of Six's, and several miles northwest of the Lower Agency. Little Crow had a two story frame house located on a bluff, one mile west of Crow's Creek. However, when the majority of Little Six's men arrived in the early hours of August 18, Crow might in fact have been asleep in a buffalo skin tepee, rather than his house.

The warriors clamored about demanding that since a massacre had already started, they should continue it, and that Little Crow should put on his war paint and lead them. But Little Crow, who had recently lost a Mdewakanton chief speakership election to Traveling Hail, fired back, "Why do you come to me for advice? Go to the man you elected speaker and let him tell you what to do." He went on to say that the murderers should be turned over to the military at Fort Ridgely. By one account he smeared black soot on his face, as though in mourning, and retired to his lodge.

The warriors, however, were crazed with excitement and their long-harbored resentments against the whites, and began cutting Crow's lodge walls with their knives. They said again that this was the time to fight--to regain their lands and avenge the thievery and insults of the traders and agents; that they would not turn over their men to "be killed like worms"; that they would rather fight. Others added that the agent had abandoned them with all of his employees and had gone off to the war--their payment had not been made; that now was the time to strike. Crow said that he did not want to kill the whites, but would go to the agency and tell the traders to leave. But the crowd began chanting, "Kill the whites and kill all these cuthairs who will not join us." Finally, someone called Crow a coward.

Now, a Dakota warrior usually could not tolerate being called either a woman, a child, a dog, or a coward, and Little Crow was no exception. With sweat forming on his forehead, he grabbed the headdress off his insulter and made his address. War with the whites hung in the balance. He first defended his war record, and then proceeded to rebuke the warriors for their naive war plans. However, too many years of disappointment, frustration, and injustice had taken their toll on him. Although vigorously opposed to making war, he eventually and irreversibly decided to fight. The speech was remembered by Little Crow's son, Wowinapa, who years later dictated it to Hanford Gordon, who translated it with the assistance of Stephen Riggs. It is doubtless the greatest and most important speech ever given by a Dakota. In it, Little Crow refers to himself as Taoyateduta, which is his personal name and means "His (Strong) Red Nation."

> **Taoyateduta is not a coward, and he is not a fool! When did he run away from his enemies? When did he leave his braves behind him on the warpath and turn back to his tepees? When you retreated from your enemies, he walked behind on your trail with his face to the Ojibways, and**

covered your backs as a she-bear covers her cubs.

Is Taoyateduta without scalps? Look at his war feathers! Behold the scalplocks of his enemies hanging there on his lodgepoles! Do they call him a coward? Taoyateduta is not a coward and he is not a fool.

Braves, you are like little children; you know not what you are doing. You are full of the white man's devil water. You are like dogs in the hot moon, when they run and snap at their own shadows. We are only little herds of buffalo left scattered; the great herds that once covered the prairies are no more. See! The white men are like locusts when they fly so thick that the whole sky is a snowstorm. You may kill one, two, ten; yes, as many as the leaves in the forest yonder, and their brothers will not miss them. Kill one, kill two, kill ten, and ten times ten will come to you. Count on your fingers all day long and white men with guns in their hands will come faster than you can count.

Yes, they fight amongst themselves a way off. Do you hear the thunder of their big guns? No, it would take you two moons to run down to where they are fighting, and all the way your path would be among white soldiers as thick as tamaracks in the swamps of the Ojibways. Yes, they fight among themselves, but if you strike at them they will all turn on you and devour you and your women and little children just as the locusts in their time fall on the trees and devour all the leaves in one day.

You are fools. You cannot see the face of your chief; your eyes are full of smoke. You cannot hear his voice; your ears are full of roaring waters. Braves, you are little children, you are fools. You will die like rabbits when the hungry wolves hunt them in the Hard Moon. Taoyateduta is not a coward. He will die with you!

Afterwards, Little Crow left with the warriors of Six's band and his own, and headed down towards the agency, as it was almost daylight. Just north of the agency, the group halted to await reinforcements from the Big Eagle and Mankato bands, whose villages were nearby (There was no time to notify the Wabasha and Wakute bands which lived south of the agency.) As the warriors congregated, another council was held. By that time a majority of those present wanted to kill not only the whites but also the mixed-bloods (though many resolved to save their particular friends). Then, both on foot and on horseback, the warriors continued down to the traders' stores. Some explained to bystanders that they were looking for Chippewas. Soon after daybreak the warriors began entering the stores--the first shot was fired by Many Hail, who killed clerk James Lynd. Winnebago Chief Little Priest, who had been visiting among the Dakotas for several weeks, was on hand, and he and his men killed the much hated trader, Andrew Myrick. According to Big Eagle, Little Crow "directed the operations." Within the next few weeks raids took place over the whole surrounding area, and Little Crow led large numbers of warriors against Fort Ridgely and New Ulm.

Sources: Antoine J. Campbell account in *Mankato Weekly Record*, Feb. 21, 1863; Wowinapa account, in Hanford L. Gordon, *Indian Legends and Other Poems* (Salem: Salem Press, 1910), 382-83; Big Eagle account in Holcombe, "A Sioux Story," 388; Thomas A. Robertson, "Reminiscences of Thomas A. Robertson," manuscript in MHS. Most accounts of this council say that it took place in Crow's house, based mainly on Big Eagle's story. However, Big Eagle may not have been present for the council, and his story was given some thirty years after the fact. Wowinapa, who was present at the council, indicates that Crow was using his lodge at the time, and he gave his account sometime before Riggs's death in 1883; Campbell, although not present at the council, gave an account of it mentioning Crow's lodge in early 1863.

"I can see...the stream of blood you are about to pour upon the bosom of this mother of ours."

TAMAHA   **August 18, 1862**

TAMAHA was probably the oldest living man among the Dakotas in 1862. He was thought to have been born sometime in the late 1750s--old enough to have fought alongside of the great Wabasha I in the American Revolutionary War. As a middle-aged man, he achieved distinction for serving the American cause in the War of 1812. Though he had become old by Dakota standards, he led a war party of Dakotas against the Sac and Fox in the Black Hawk War of 1832. More incredibly, he took part in fights with the Chippewas in 1842 (at Kaposia), at Apple River in 1850, and again at Shakopee in 1858. Although it can be proved that Tamaha was alive in 1862, Charles Eastman is the only source to state that he was present for the crucial war council of August 18. (As Eastman's father, Many Lightnings, attended that council, it is probable that it was he who spoke of Tamaha and re-called Tamaha's speech.) The old medicine man and war prophet gave advice based on an incredible lifetime of experiences:

> **What! What! is this Little Crow? Is that Little Six? You, too, White Dog [the former Farmer chief], are you here? I cannot see well now, but I can see you with my mind's eye the stream of blood you are about to pour upon the bosom of this mother of ours.**
>
> **I stand before you on three legs, but the third leg [referring to his staff] has brought me much wisdom. I have traveled much; I have visited the people whom you think to defy. This means the total surrender of our beautiful land, the land of a thousand lakes and streams. Methinks you are about to commit an act like that of the porcupine, who climbs a tree, balances himself upon a springy bough, and then gnaws off the very bough upon which he is sitting; hence when it gives way, he falls upon the sharp rocks below.**
>
> **Behold, the great Pontiac, whose grave I saw near St. Louis; he was murdered while an exile from his own country! Think of the brave Black Hawk! Methinks his spirit is still wailing through Wisconsin and Illinois for his lost people! I do not say you have no cause to complain, but to resist is self-destruction. I am done.**

Tamaha's prophecies proved correct. No sooner had the Dakotas been defeated when Congress abrogated all treaties with them and thus appropriated all Dakota lands and goods. Tamaha was among the Dakotas who surrendered to Colonel Henry Sibley's forces in the fall of 1862. He was shipped with others to Crow Creek, Dakota Territory, in the spring of 1863, where he and a great number soon died of malnutrition and disease.

Sources: Mark Diedrich, "Tamaha, 'The One-Eyed Sioux,' One Hundred Years in the Life of a Dakota Medi-cine Man," an unpublished manuscript, ca. 1982; Charles A. Eastman, *Indian Heroes and Great Chieftains* (Boston: Little, Brown, and Co., 1918), 66-67.

"I would slaughter such 'braves' as you are, as I might kill beavers on dry land."

AKIPA   **August 23, 1862**

AKIPA (MEETING), also called His Big Voiced Pipe (Tacandupahotanka), was a Wahpeton chief. He had been a great warrior in his day and boasted eighteen feathers in his war bonnet. He also served his people as a physician, having considerable knowledge of diseases and remedies. Through marriage to Winona Crawford, Akipa became stepfather to Susan Frenier Brown, wife of Dakota agent Joseph Brown. Samuel Brown said that his father had tried to get his grandfather to become a "white man," but that Akipa did not like white ways. However, he eventually took up farming and joined the mission church with the adopted name--Joseph Akipa Renville.

When Akipa heard the news at Yellow Medicine that the Lower Dakotas were killing the whites, he could not have been more shocked. No one had anticipated such a thing, although Akipa had witnessed the close call on August 4, when the Upper Dakotas broke into the government warehouse and faced off against 100 soldiers. Soon after, Akipa learned that his daughter, Susan Brown, and her son, Samuel, were being held captive at Little Crow's village. Accompanied by a few warriors, he immediately drove down in his wagon to demand that they be turned over to him. Arriving on August 23, he found himself facing a wild and crazed group of Indians, who taunted him with charges of cowardice for not having joined them in the attacks on the whites--for not having killed "even a babe." Unperturbed, Akipa rebuked the men with a strong anti-war speech (which was remembered and later translated by Samuel Brown):

> There is no bravery in killing helpless men, women, and little children, who have no means of defense. That is simply cowardice, and it is only cowards who would boast of it. If I had found that any of my relatives had been harmed by such cowards, I would tomahawk your whole camp. I would slaughter such "braves" as you are, as I might kill beavers on dry land.
> When the sun arose that witnessed the horrors of indiscriminate massacre of the whites in this valley of the Minnesota, regardless of sex or age, by you Lower Sioux, the upper bands were peacefully attending to their crops on their own reservation, or out on the distant prairies hunting buffalo. The report of that awful bloody day's work fell on our ears with more astounding force than the voice of the Great Spirit issuing from the black clouds of the west.

Akipa then spoke at length on the great power of the whites (which he had seen first-hand during his 1858 trip to Washington), and the imbecility of a few hundred Dakotas going against them. Samuel Brown felt that Akipa's defiant speech was one of the bravest acts he had ever seen.

Sources: Hughes, *Indian Chiefs*, 89-92; Samuel J. Brown, interview by Folwell, August 1, 1908, Notebooks, Folwell Papers. Akipa died at the Sisseton Reservation in South Dakota in 1891.

"I am a Dakota Indian, born and reared in the midst of evil."

JOHN OTHER DAY   **August 26, 1862**

JOHN OTHER DAY was a great drunkard most of his life, and while drunk had killed three or four men. However, during the 1850s he was converted by the missionaries, and became a leader among the so-called "civilized" Wahpetons at Yellow Medicine. He cut his hair, wore white man's clothes, and adopted farming as an occupation. During the 1858 trip to Washington he met and married a white woman, who returned with him to the reservation. Other Day attributed his change of character to his conversion: "It is the religion of Jesus Christ alone; but for this, I should have been the bloodiest of the murderers."

When news of the outbreak reached the Wahpetons, Other Day determined to lead as many of the whites at the Upper Agency as possible to safety. Over fifty people followed him in a flight across the western Minnesota prairies, eventually arriving safely at Shakopee. Other Day went on to St. Paul where he was honored at a ceremony at Ingersoll's Hall. For the occasion, he prepared the following statement which was translated and written down by Gideon H. Pond:

> I am a Dakota Indian, born and reared in the midst
> of evil. I grew up without the knowledge of any
> good thing. I have been instructed by Americans,
> and taught to read and write. This I found to be
> good. I became acquainted with the Sacred Writings,
> and there learned my vileness.
>
> At the present time I have fallen into great
> evil and affliction, but have escaped from it; and
> with fifty-four men, women, and children, without
> moccasins, without food, and without a blanket,
> I have arrived in the midst of a great people, and
> now my heart is glad. I attribute it to the mercy
> of the Great Spirit.

(Stephen Riggs, who was with the party, however, later wrote that Other Day's rescue of the whites was in large measure due to the urgings of his white wife.) Other Day afterwards served as a scout for Colonel Sibley and fought against Little Crow's forces at Wood Lake. The government rewarded him with $2,500 in 1866. He eventually rejoined his people on the Sisseton Reservation near Fort Wadsworth and died there of tuberculosis at age fifty on October 30, 1869.

Sources: Hughes, *Indian Chiefs*, 78-79; Henry H. Sibley, "Sketch of John Other Day," *Minnesota Historical Collections*, 3 (1880):99-102; speech in *St. Paul Pioneer and Democrat*, August 27, 1862.

"If the young braves have pushed the white men, I have done this myself."

LITTLE CROW   September 7, 1862

AFTER A DAKOTA VICTORY at Birch Coulie, a note was found on the battle-field addressed to Little Crow from Colonel Henry H. Sibley. Asked if he had any propositions to make, Little Crow composed a letter which was interpreted and drafted by A. J. Campbell. He firstly justified the war with statments about Galbraith, inferring that the agent's non-issue of goods at the Lower Agency was the major cause. Secondly, he blamed various traders for their insulting remarks, and he believed that leading trader Louis Robert was conspiring to defraud the Dakotas. It was well known that for some weeks the traders were commonly telling the Dakotas that they could not purchase food on credit and that they would be forced to "eat grass." And a personal letter written by Andrew Myrick reveals that there were rumors that Robert wanted to form a secret partnership with Galbraith to take exclusive control over the Indian trade--that the agent could realize "at least $10,000 a year" by such a scheme. Little Crow also wanted Sibley to know that the Winnebagoes shared in the responsibility for the war. He did not elaborate on this, but Little Priest and Leader (the son of Winnishiek) had fought with the Dakotas at Fort Ridgely and New Ulm, and they had promised to send Crow their families while they and their warriors attacked Mankato--however, their attempt to gain any substantial support from their tribe was futile. Still, Little Crow did not shrink from stating that the primary responsibility for the war rested on his own shoulders.

> Yellow Medicine
> Sept. 7, 1862
>
> Dear Sir:
>
> For what reason we have commenced this war, I will
> tell you. It is on account of Major Galbraith, we made
> a treaty with the Government, and beg for what little we
> do get, and then can't get it till our children are dieing
> [sic] with hunger. It was with the traders that commence
> [it] Mr. A. J. Myrick told the Indians they would eat grass
> or their own dung, then Mr. Forbes told the lower Sioux
> that [they] were not men, then Robert he was making
> with his friends to defraud us o[ut] of our money, if the
> young braves have push the white men, I have done this
> myself; So I want you to let the Governor Ramsey know
> this. I have a great many prisoners, women and children,
> it ain't all our fault the Winnebagoes was in the engagement,
> two of them was killed. I want you to give me answer by
> bearer all at present.
>
> > Yours truly,
> > Friend Little (x) Crow

Lt. Timothy Sheehan, who had been at the Upper Agency through the summer, and who helped defend Fort Ridgely, wrote in his diary that day: "Little Crow sent in a flag of truce with a letter to Col. Sibley stating that Galbraith, Forbes, and the traders were the cause of the war. My opinion is the same."

Sources: Harriet E. McConkey, *Dakota War Whoop* (St. Paul: D. D. Merrill, 1863), 210; on Robert, see Andrew Myrick to Nathan Myrick, July 26, 1862, and William L. Quinn testimony, in Sioux Claims, Special Files, no. 274, National Archives; on Winnebagoes, see *Mankato Weekly Record*, Feb. 21, 1863; Timothy Sheehan Diary, Sept. 7, 1862, Sheehan Papers, MHS.

"Little Crow has now got himself into trouble that we know he can never get himself out of...."

TAOPI   September 10, 1862

TAOPI, OR WOUNDED MAN, was a member of Little Crow's band until 1861 when he was appointed chief of the Lower Sioux farmer band by agent Galbraith. The new chief, like others among the Wahpetons, had converted to Christianity, believing as well that he should abandon his traditional culture and religion. When Bishop Henry Whipple visited the agency in June 1861, Taopi, along with Wabasha and Good Thunder, invited him to establish a mission among them: "We are looking into a grave. We hear you come from the Great Spirit to help His poor children."

However, Taopi's stand for becoming a "white man," cutting his hair, and wearing pantaloons instead of a breechcloth, brought him into confrontation with Little Crow, who was a pronounced opponent of the agents' acculturation programs. Gideon Pond, who by that time was a rather embittered old missionary, referred to Little Crow as one "who, from old time, had been the open and determined enemy of the Christian religion, and a most zealous and devoted worshipper of the Taku Wakan [Something Holy or Mysterious--a general, inclusive name for the Dakota gods]...." The war brought the two men into conflict again.

The attack on the Lower Agency on August 18 took the Farmer band by surprise. By the time they were aware of what was happening, the hostile Dakotas arrived to force them to don their Indian dress and join them. Taopi, however, began to look for a way in which he might help the whites, particularly the captives which were taken during the war. On September 10 he risked his life by sending the following communication to Colonel Sibley:

> **You know that Little Crow has been opposed to me in everything that our people have had to do with the whites. He has been opposed to everything in the form of civilization or Christianity. I have always been in favor of, and of late years, have done everything of the kind that has been offered to us by the government and other good white people--he has now got himself into trouble that we know he can never get himself out of, and he is trying to involve those few of us that are still the friend of the American in the murder of the poor whites that have been settled in the border, but I have been kept back by threats that I should be killed if I did anything to help the whites; but if you will now appoint some place for me to meet you, myself and the few friends that I have will get all the prisoners we can, and with our family, go to whatever place you will appoint for us to meet.**

Sources: Samuel Hinman to Whipple, Aug. 5, 1862, Whipple Papers; Whipple, *Lights and Shadows*, 111-12; Gideon H. Pond, "Dakota Superstition," *Minnesota Historical Collections*, 2 (1867):225; Mark F. Diedrich, "Christian Taopi: Farmer Chief of the Mdewakanton Dakota," *Minnesota Archaeologist*, 40 (June 1981): 65-77. Captive George Spencer said that from mid-September on, Little Crow threatened him, Taopi, and His Thunder (or Chaska) with death. McConkey, *Dakota War Whoop*, 234.

LITTLE PAUL MAZAKUTEMANI

"Why did you not tell us you were going to kill them?"

LITTLE PAUL   September 1862

MOST OF THE LEADERS of the Upper Dakotas were very bitter about the fact
that they had not been consulted about the proposed war on the whites prior to
the actual fact. Many of the chiefs had been to Washington and knew that the
Dakotas would have to pay a terrible price for their war folly. Other leaders were
appalled because they considered themselves as "white men." When Little Crow
and the Lower Dakotas retreated to the upper reservation, many councils took
place between the pro-war and anti-war factions. Little Paul, the chief speaker of
the Upper Dakotas, was the most prolific in his attempts to persuade the Dakotas
to give up the war and give up the captives. In his apparent first speech on the
matter, he said:

> I am going to tell you what I think and what I am
> ready to do, now and hereafter. You Mdewakanton
> and Wahpekute Indians have been with the white
> men a great deal longer than the Upper Indians. Yet I,
> who am an Upper Indian, have put on white men's
> clothes, and consider myself now a white man. I was
> very much surprised to hear that you had been killing
> the settlers, for you have had the advice of preachers
> for so many years. Why did you not tell us you were
> going to kill them? I ask you the question again, Why
> did you not tell us? You make no answer. The reason
> was, if you had done so, and we had counseled to-
> gether, you would not have been able to have involved
> our young men with you. When we older men heard of
> it, we were so surprised that we knew not what to do.
> By your involving our young men without consulting
> us you have done us a great injustice.
>
> I am now going to tell you something you don't like.
> You have gotten our people into this difficulty through
> your incitements to its rash young soldiers without a
> council being called and our consent being obtained, and
> I shall use all the means I can to get them out of it with-
> out reference to you.
>
> I am opposed to their continuing this war, or of
> committing further outrages, and I warn you not to do it.
> I have heard a great many of you say that you were brave
> men and could whip the whites. This is a lie. Persons who
> will cut women and children's throats are squaws and cow-
> ards.
>
> You say the whites are not brave. You will see. They
> will not, it is true, kill women and children, as you have done,
> but they will fight you who have arms in your hands.
>
> I am ashamed of the way you have acted toward the cap-
> tives. Fight the whites if you desire to, but do it like brave men.
> Give me the captives and I will carry them to Fort Ridgely. I
> hear one of you say that if I take them, there are soldiers [who]
> will shoot me. I will take the risk. I am not afraid of death, but
> I am opposed to the way you act toward the prisoners. If any of
> you have the feelings of men, you will give them up. You may look
> as fierce at me as you please, but I shall ask you once, twice, and
> ten times to deliver these women and children to their friends.

Source: *Minnesota in the Civil and Indian Wars*, 2 vols. (St. Paul, 1891), 1:742-43.

"...let the prisoners die with us."

RATTLING RUNNER   September 1862

WHEN LITTLE PAUL spoke out against the war, Rattling Runner defended the
continuance of it. He was a member of Little Crow's band, a leader of the Soldiers'
Lodge, and the son-in-law of Wabasha--he therefore had substantial influence. He
had taken a leading role in the battles and was particularly singled out (later) for
having urged the warriors forward in the fight at New Ulm.

Rattling Runner was an obviously intelligent and clearheaded young Dakota. His
speech reveals that he had reflected a great deal on past injustices the Dakotas had
endured from the whites. For years they had complained about their agents, particularly Joseph Brown, who they felt had been robbing them. He recalled, as well,
many instances in which Dakota warriors had been imprisoned for various offenses--
mainly for carrying on a defensive warfare with the Chippewas (Instances of this
had occurred in 1850, 1852, 1853, 1855 and 1856.) In 1854 Uhazy had been hung
in St. Paul (for killing a white woman). In 1853 a Dakota had been shot mistakenly
by William Dodd (who was killed at New Ulm). In 1855 Young Chief Sleepy Eyes
had been shot and clubbed by soldiers. With these things in mind, Rattling Runner
made the following bold statements:

> I am for continuing the war, and am opposed to the
> delivery of the prisoners. I have no confidence that
> the whites will stand by any agreement they make if
> we give them up. Ever since we treated with them,
> their agents and traders have robbed and cheated us.
> Some of our people have been shot, some hung; others
> placed upon floating ice and drowned; and many have
> been starved in their prisons.
>   It was not the intention of the nation to kill any
> of the whites until after the few returned from Acton
> and told what they had done. When they did this, all
> the young men became excited, and commenced the
> massacre. The older ones would have prevented it if
> they could, but since the treaties, they have lost all
> their influence. We may regret what has happened
> but the matter has gone too far to be remedied. We
> have got to die. Let us, then, kill as many of the whites
> as possible, and let the prisoners die with us.

Little Paul later recalled Rattling Runner as saying to him: "The braves say they
will not give you the captives. The Mdewakantons are men, and therefore as long as
one of them lives they will not stop pointing their guns at the Americans."

Sources: Isaac V.D. Heard, *History of the Sioux War and Massacres of 1862 and 1863* (New York: Harper and
Brothers, 1863), 151-52; Stephen R. Riggs, trans. "Narrative of Paul Mazakootemane," *Minnesota Historical
Collections*, 3 (1880):85.

"...die, if die you must, with arms in your hands like warriors and braves...."

LITTLE CROW   **September 1862**

LITTLE CROW had no answer for Little Paul as to why the Lower Dakotas did not consult the Upper prior to their decision to start an all-out war. The circumstances did not even allow for leading lower chiefs, like Wabasha and Wakute, to be brought into the matter. Little Crow also sidestepped the plea for the release of the captives. Later, he did decide to release them--but for the time being the captives were Little Crow's ace in the hole for an eventual peace settlement. In replying to Little Paul, Crow chose to speak to the fact that the Dakotas were "dead men" as far as the whites were concerned, and that the only patriotic thing to do was to fight and die like warriors. Although he exaggerated about the fact that only one Sioux had been hanged by the whites in recent memory, he was quite correct in his realization as to the probable fate of most of his men. Within two months a military court would have over 300 Dakotas slated for the noose (Only President Lincoln's aversion to such an incredible mass killing prevented this from occurring.)

> Paul wants us to make peace. It is impossible to do so, if we desired. Did we ever do the most trifling thing, and the whites not hang us? Now we have been killing them by the hundreds in Dakota, Minnesota, and Iowa, and I know that if they get us into their power they will hang every one of us. As for me, I will kill as many of them as I can, and fight them till I die.
>
> Do not think you will escape. There is not a band of Indians from the Redwood Agency to Big Stone Lake that has not had some of its members embroiled in the war. I tell you we must fight and perish together. A man is a fool and a coward who thinks otherwise, and who will desert his nation at such a time? Disgrace not yourselves by a surrender to those who will hang you up like dogs, but die, if die you must with arms in your hands, like warriors and braves of the Dakota!

Sources: Heard, *History of the Sioux War*, 158-59; Uhazy was condemned for killing a Mrs. Keener on October 27, 1852; he was held in a Ramsey County Jail until his execution on December 27, 1854--although newspaper accounts do not indicate that any Dakotas witnessed the execution, it is obvious that the matter was greatly blown up in their minds--*Minnesota Weekly Times*, Dec. 29, 1854; *Minnesota Democrat* (St. Paul), Jan. 3, 1855.

"...it is just as if you had waited for me in ambush and shot me down."

STANDING BUFFALO   **September 1862**

STANDING BUFFALO was the handsome, young, principal chief of the Northern Sissetons of Lake Traverse and Big Stone Lake. He had been present at Yellow Medicine on August 4, when the Upper Dakotas broke into the government warehouse. He had counseled against violence, but agreed to stand with his people in this action because his tribe was literally starving to death. When he returned to the plains of North Dakota for a buffalo hunt, he undoubtedly assumed that the agent would placate the hunger of the Lower Dakotas. Serious trouble had seemingly been averted. However, several Wahpetons rode into his hunting camp on the Sheyenne River about two weeks later and informed him that war had broken out!

Standing Buffalo rode in from the plains and eventually spoke in a council with Little Crow in mid-September. He spoke of his shock and his fears and his outrage:

> I am a young man, but I have always felt friendly toward the whites because they were kind to my father [Orphan]. You have brought me into great danger without my knowing of it beforehand. By killing the whites it is just as if you had waited for me in ambush and shot me down. You Lower Indians feel very bad because we have all gotten into trouble; but I feel worse because I know that neither I nor my people have killed any of the whites, and that yet we have to suffer for the guilty.
>
> I was out buffalo hunting when I heard of the outbreak, and I felt as if I was dead, and feel so now. You all know that the Indians cannot live without the aid of the white man....
>
> We claim this reservation. What are you doing here? If you want to fight the whites, go back and fight them. Leave me at my village at Big Stone Lake. You sent word to my young men to come down, and that you had plenty of oxen, and horses, and goods, and powder, and lead, and now we see nothing. We are going back to Big Stone Lake, and leave you to fight the whites. Those who make peace can say that Standing Buffalo and his people will give themselves up in the spring.

Source: Diedrich, *Odyssey of Chief Standing Buffalo*, 41-43.

"I cannot account for the disgraceful defeat."

LITTLE CROW   September 23, 1862

ON SEPTEMBER 23, 1862, the last battle of the war in Minnesota was fought at Wood Lake. Little Crow mustered some 738 Dakotas for an attack on Sibley's army of 1,600. However, many of the Dakotas opposed the war and positioned themselves where they would not have to take an active part in the fight. Thus, although the Dakotas fought valiantly, they could not overpower the whites, some of whom were Civil War veterans, who were aided as well by the mixed-blood company of volunteers (which agent Galbraith had raised) called the Renville Rangers. The Dakotas lost about nineteen killed--their worst casualties of any fight during the war--and Sibley lost seven killed and thirty-four wounded. The Dakotas left the field in disorder--but Sibley did not press his victory. Back at camp, Little Crow (according to captive Samuel Brown) was despondent and almost heartbroken. He stepped outside of his lodge and said in a loud voice:

> I am ashamed to call myself a Sioux. Seven hundred picked warriors whipped by the cowardly whites. Better run away and scatter out over the plains like buffalo and wolves. To be sure the whites had big guns and better arms than the Indians and outnumbered us four or five to one, but that is no reason we should not have whipped them, for we are brave men, while they are cowardly women. I cannot account for the disgraceful defeat. It must be the work of traitors in our midst.

Indeed, A. J. Campbell, who was in Little Crow's camp, later stated that the greater part of the Indian force did not take part in the fight at all. Afterwards, Little Crow tried to convince the Dakotas to move up in a body to Fort Garry and place themselves under the protection of the British--but a majority had resolved to remain behind and surrender to Sibley. Campbell, who visited Sibley after the battle, came back to ask Little Crow to give up the captives. Crow agreed to do so, saying that if they killed them "the whites would then follow us to the end of the earth and give us no peace until they exterminate us. It would be cruel and cowardly too, and I will save their lives and let them go back to their friends." Then Campbell advised Crow to give himself up. But to this the chief said that the whites were so angry with him, that if they got him in their power they would "cut him to pieces and boil him in a kettle"; therefore, he would fight to the last. He then begged the Dakotas, with tears in his eyes, to join him in a war to the end--that if they stayed behind, the whites would punish them even if they were innocent.

Sources: Samuel J. Brown, "In Captivity," in 56 Congress, 2 session, *Senate Document*, 23 (1900):21; McConkey, *Dakota War Whoop*, 130-31; Campbell account in *Mankato Weekly Record*, Feb. 21, 1863; Celia Campbell Stay reminiscences, in Alex Siefurt Papers, MHS.

MARK DIEDRICH 1987

STANDING BUFFALO

CHAPTER SIX

POST—WAR PERIOD, OCTOBER 1862-1874

"I never shall have a home until I sleep in the grave."

"We will fight until we drop dead!"

WHITE LODGE   circa October 1862

WHITE LODGE (WAKIYASKA) became the leading Southern Sisseton chief after the breakup of the Old Sleepy Eyes' band in the early 1850s. He and his band refused to take up residence on the Dakota reservation. Although he was instrumental in getting the Upper Dakotas to join in the expedition against Inkpaduta in the summer of 1857, he apparently grew increasingly upset with the whites. When war broke out, White Lodge threw himself wholeheartedly into it. He and his band attacked and killed a great number of settlers at Lake Shetek. With some fifteen captives, he rejoined Little Crow's following for a time. But sometime before the battle at Wood Lake, he took his people, including members of the Lean Bear and Young Sleepy Eyes bands, westward to the Missouri River. Arriving there about October 18, they camped at Swan Lake, about one hundred miles north of Fort Pierre. A number of Yanktonais came into White Lodge's camp to purchase the white captives, wishing to give them freedom. At first White Lodge refused to consider the suggestions of the Yanktonais (who had been dubbed "Fool Soldiers" by their own people) and made the following declarations about the war against the whites in Minnesota:

> We come from the east where the sky is made red by the fires which burn the homes of the whites, and the ground is red with the blood of the whites that the Santees are killing. These white captives we have taken after killing many of the people. We will not again be friends to the whites. We have done a bad thing and now we will keep on doing bad things. We will not give up the captives. We will fight until we drop dead.

Although the chief was later induced to give up his captives, he was never induced to give up his war. He kept on the run with his band and took refuge in the British Possessions when necessary to escape American soldiers. By one account he was with Inkpaduta at the Battle of the Little Big Horn in 1876. He apparently died soon afterwards in Canada.

Sources: Robinson, *Dakota History*, 308-9; McConkey, *Dakota War Whoop*, 237; W. A. Burleigh to Commissioner William P. Dole, Nov. 17, 1862, in *Report of the Commissioner of Indian Affairs* (Washington: Government Printing Office, 1863), 376; Diedrich, *Famous Chiefs*, 55.

"...we ask our Great Father to let us live...."

SURRENDERED CHIEFS and HEADMEN   December 19, 1862

AFTER THE BATTLE OF WOOD LAKE, some 1,700 Dakotas surrendered to
Colonel Henry Sibley at "Camp Release." The men were then tricked into giving
up their weapons. Many were tried before a military court and sentenced to death
by hanging. Those who were considered innocent, including the elderly, and the
women and children were sent under the charge of agent Galbraith to dig potatoes
at Yellow Medicine. In mid-October they were moved to Redwood Agency, and
on November 7 Lt. Col. William R. Marshall marched them to Fort Snelling.
A large "pen" was erected below the fort on the Minnesota River to enclose the
Dakota camp, which was guarded by soldiers on the perimeter. Even embittered
white visitors were appalled by the terrible conditions in the camp, finding among
other things that the paths between the lodges were "the receptacles of all the
offal." On December 19, as the state was preparing to conduct a mass execution
of thirty-eight Dakotas at Mankato, the imprisoned chiefs and headmen at Fort
Snelling composed the following statement, which was interpreted by Antoine
D. Frenier and apparently written down by agent Galbraith. It was signed by
such leaders as Wabasha, Wakute, Red Legs (the Wahpekute chief), Taopi, Traveling Hail, Little Paul Mazakutemani, John Other Day, and Spirit Walker. It is
of particular interest that they gave the cause of the war to have been government
favoritism of the acculturated Indians (Policies enforced by agents Brown and Galbraith had virtually disenfranchised all of the traditionally-minded Indians from
treaty benefits.)

Last August our young men all broke out and
butchered a great many white men and women and
children. The cause that they did this was that many
of us had commenced to live as white men, and they
were jealous of us; and on that account they went to
war....We killed nobody. We helped to save the captives,
and we succeeded in saving nearly three hundred white
women and children....
    We are farmers, and want that our Great Father
would allow us to farm again whenever he pleases, only
we never want to go away with the wild blanket Indians
again; for what we have done for the whites they would
kill us....we of the Lower Sioux would like to go back
to our farms, and there live as white men, or we would
like to live among the white men, and farm as they do,
if they would let us.
    We think we ought to be dealt with as our Great
Father does with his white children: the bad ought to
be punished, and the good to be well-treated. All the
Indians who were engaged in killing the white men and
women and children should be hanged; but we who did
not do bad hope to live, and we ask our Great Father to
let us live and to aid us. We think we have not forfeited
our annuities or other funds, because we have done no
wrong; and we ask that such way as to him seems best
for our good, to help us to live....

Sources: McConkey, *Dakota War Whoop*, 277; *Congressional Globe* (Washington), Jan. 26, 1863.

"...today I am set apart for execution...."

RATTLING RUNNER   **December 24, 1862**

AFTER WOOD LAKE, Wabasha and Rattling Runner joined Little Crow in his flight
to the Red River. However, Wabasha soon after turned back, and convinced his son-
in-law to do the same. Later, Wabasha was sent with the "friendly Sioux" to Fort
Snelling, but Rattling Runner was tried by the military court and sentenced to death.
Although President Lincoln reduced the number of those to be executed from about
three hundred down to thirty-eight, Rattling Runner was among those still on the
list. While most of the condemned men were convicted for murdering civilians or
rape, Rattling Runner was only guilty of participating in the major battles of the
war. Bitter about this turn of events, he dictated a letter (translated and written
down by Stephen Riggs) to his father-in-law, who had convinced him to surrender:

> Wabasha, you have deceived me. You told me that if we
> followed the advice of Gen. Sibley, and give [sic] ourselves
> up to the whites, all would be well, no innocent man would be
> injured. I have not killed, wounded, or injured a white man, or
> any other person. I have not participated in the plunder of their
> property; and yet today I am set apart for execution and must die
> in a few days, while men who are guilty remain in prison. My wife
> is your daughter, my children are your grandchildren. I leave them
> all in your care and under your protection. Do not let them suffer,
> and when my children are grown up let them know that their father
> died because he followed the advice of his chief, and without having
> the blood of a white man to answer for to the Great Spirit.
>   My wife and children are dear to me. Let them not grieve for
> me. Let them remember that the brave should be prepared to meet
> death, and I will do so as becomes a Dakota.

On December 26 the condemned painted their faces and were addressed by Augustin
Ravoux. The Indians broke into their death songs as their arms were pinioned with
cords and their wrists were tied in front. A reporter commented that the effect of
the death songs was "magical"--that it seemed as if "they had passed in spirit through
the valley of the shadow of death, and already had their eyes fixed on the pleasant
hunting grounds beyond." At ten o'clock they were marched from the prison to
a huge scaffold upon which they were all to stand together in one group to be hung
enmasse. Nooses were placed about their necks and white hoods were placed upon
their heads. Many held hands with their companions and others called out their
own names and were answered by their friends. Colonel Stephen Miller then gave
the order for the proceedings to begin: Major Joseph Brown (the former agent)
played three slow measured beats on a drum, and Lake Shetek survivor, William
Duley (whose wife had been a captive of White Lodge's), struck the platform
rope with an axe--the first blow failed to sever it. With the second swing, the
trapdoor opened and the thirty-eight Dakotas fell to their deaths. Rattling Runner
died instantly, but his rope broke and his body fell to the ground--he was hung up
again. Others died with their hands still clasped to their neighbor's. A large number
of white onlookers cheered at first, but then went silent upon seeing the bodies
dangling in the air. It was the largest mass hanging ever in the United States. One
or two of the executed, due to name confusion, turned out to be the wrong men.
Stephen Riggs, who had aided in the trials, later said that "many were condemned
to death on insufficient evidence....the excitement and exasperation of the times un-
fitted us for doing justice to the Indians."

Sources: Heard, *History of the Sioux War*, 284; McConkey, *Dakota War Whoop*, 300-3, 238-39; *Mankato Weekly Record*, Feb. 21, 1863; *St. Paul Pioneer*, Dec. 28, 1862, May 22, 1864. By one account, it was Cut Nose's rope which broke.

"Tell them not to shoot me in my tepee like a dog."

TAOPI   **circa Summer 1863**

TAOPI, THE FORMER FARMER CHIEF, was among the Dakotas who were held
at Fort Snelling through the spring of 1863. Due to Bishop Whipple's intervention,
he was excused from being sent to the Crow Creek Reservation in Dakota Territory;
he was afraid that he would suffer retaliation from various Indians for his having
helped the whites. He and a few others were allowed to camp on Alexander Faribault's farm at Faribault. However, despite Taopi's reputation for having helped
rescue white captives, anti-Sioux sentiment was so strong that his life was threatened
by local people. Taopi wrote to his sponsor:

> My father, read this paper. It tells you how I
> saved your people from death. If your white
> brothers have the same law as savage Indians,
> that when a man is killed, some one of the mur-
> derous race must die, and they wish for this to
> take my life, tell them not to shoot me in my
> tepee like a dog. Ask them to send for me, and
> I will show them how an innocent man can die.

Whipple and Faribault had the statement published in the newspaper, and the excitement in the town died down.

Source: Diedrich, "Christian Taopi," 73.

"...he and his men were then fighting with the ropes round their necks...."

LITTLE CROW   June 1863

AFTER LEAVING MINNESOTA, Little Crow labored heroically to unite the various Sioux and other tribes into a confederacy to fight the Americans. But everywhere divided opinions frustrated his efforts. He finally sought the assistance of the British at Fort Garry (Winnipeg), arriving on May 29, 1863 with a band of eighty people. For the occasion of his visit, he wore a black coat with velvet collar, a breechcloth of fine blue material, costly shawls about his waist and as a turban about his head, deerskin leggings and moccasins inwrought with fancy beadwork, and in his belt, he carried a six-shooter revolver. A newspaper reporter commented that the chief's oratory was "the lever by which he controls his followers and bends their stubborn wills to his purposes," that his eloquence was "matchless" in council--"His genius in making the worse appear the better reason--his command of logic--his slippery utterances--his bold and wholesale lying when necessary, challenge wonder and admiration...."

It was a critical time for the hostile Dakotas. Without assistance they would be extremely handicapped in continuing the war. Unfortunately, Crow's exact speech was not recorded, but the substance was written down in an account by historian Joseph Hargrave as follows:

> Little Crow stated his desire to be on friendly terms with the English, whose allies his people had been during the Anglo-American war, and whose flags and medals of the reign of George the Third, men of his band carried.... He said that, during the time of the war alluded to, the British had told his people that whenever they should get into trouble with the Americans they had only to come and the folds of the red flag of the north would wrap them round, and preserve them from their enemies. He had come to claim the fulfillment of this promise.
>
> His people had suffered much for years; good faith had not been kept with them; they had been defrauded of their own, and advantage was then being taken of the rash behavior of their young braves to gain a pretence for exterminating them. He knew he and his men were then fighting with the ropes round their necks, and their only safety lay in waging a truceless war. Already he had been deceived by a piece of sharp practice in which he had been unfairly induced to give up American prisoners in his possession under pretext of effecting an exchange, whereas his friends in the hands of the enemy had been hanged.
>
> He begged Governor [Alexander G.] Dallas to exert his influence on his behalf with General Sibley....He wished the General to come to terms with him, but added if he refused to do so, the Indians must fight in righteous self-defense....

Dallas agreed to transmit Little Crow's message to Sibley, but otherwise held out no hope to the beleaguered chief. Disheartened, but still determined, Little Crow walked back to Minnesota to capture horses. But while eating berries near Hutchinson, he was ambushed and killed by a farmer and his son on July 3, 1863. He was arguably the greatest eastern Dakota orator and war leader!

Sources: Joseph J. Hargrave, *Red River* (Montreal: John Lovell, 1871), 290-92; *Nor'Wester* (Winnipeg), Aug. 5, 1863; Diedrich, *Famous Chiefs*, 74-75.

"...maybe it is to fool us that they sent you...."

SISSETON CHIEFS   December 22, 1863

MANY OF THE NORTHERN SISSETONS had hoped to surrender to General
Sibley in the spring of 1863. Their leading chief, Standing Buffalo, asked Governor
Alexander Dallas of Fort Garry to send Sibley a message in this regard. However,
spring dragged into summer, and the Sissetons, along with most of the refugee
Minnesota Dakotas were forced to go buffalo hunting in order to survive. While
hunting near Big Mound (North Dakota) in late July, they were surprised to learn
that General Sibley and his army were quickly approaching their camp. A battle
ensued, but after dark, Standing Buffalo and most of his people separated from
the other Dakotas and headed north. That winter they sought refuge on British
Territory. In December the chiefs learned that Sibley had sent Father Alexis
Andre on a peace mission to them. Standing Buffalo had previously met the
priest, who served the Red River Metis, and was prone to trust a "black robe."
A meeting with Andre was arranged at End of the Woods, on the Assiniboine
River. Andre informed a group of chiefs and headmen of Sibley's surrender
terms--but held back from telling them that the general demanded that all murderers
of white people be given up to him as a precondition of making peace. They
made the following reply:

> We believe in your words, for you have pity on
> us, and lies do not cross your lips--it is not the
> Black Robe who will betray us--but you know
> how deceitful and [what] liars the Americans
> are. Your heart is too good to realize how bad
> theirs is--you are sincere but who can assure us
> of the sincerity of the Americans. Maybe it is
> to fool us that they sent you, for we would not
> have listened to anybody else but you. If traders
> or others had been sent to talk to us of peace, we
> would have ignored them as passing little birds,
> or little dogs barking at our doors, and we would
> not have paid any attention to their words. We
> will take council on what you have just told us.

However, soon after the council, the Dakotas received news that American troops
under Major Edwin Hatch at Pembina had killed two Sioux women and their children
near St. Joseph. They could not understand how this could have occurred if the
Americans were serious about making peace.

Sources: Alexis Andre to Bishop Alexander Tache, Dec. 29, 1863, Belleau Collection, Provincial Archives of
Manitoba (Winnipeg); Diedrich, *Odyssey of Chief Standing Buffalo*, 57-58.

"...you are a very little man to talk to a great chief like me...."

LITTLE SIX   January 16, 1864

AFTER THE DEATH OF LITTLE CROW, Little Six became the leading hostile Mdewakanton chief. Due to fights with generals Henry Sibley and Alfred Sully in the summer of 1863, Little Six took his following north into British Territory. Governor Dallas visited Little Six and later reported that he found these six hundred Sioux "in a state of absolute starvation, destitute of clothing, or any of the necessaries of life," subsisting on carrion and jackfish. As far as the Dakotas were concerned, they were going to die of starvation, and they preferred to die near the settlements so that the settlers "might put their women and children under the ice," --that is, bury them.

In the meantime, a battalion of U.S. cavalry under Major Edwin Hatch was stationed at Pembina to either fight or receive the surrender of the Sioux. Hatch and a few others made plans to kidnap the notorious Little Six, and Medicine Bottle, and carry them across the international boundary line to Pembina. By mid-January 1864 John H. McKenzie, a U. S. citizen, who lived at Fort Garry, set out to bring the scheme to fruition. On January 16, 1864, Little Six and Medicine Bottle attended a council with McKenzie at Lane's trading post, twenty-five miles west of Fort Garry. Through interpreter Onisime Giguere, McKenzie tried to persuade the chief and his friend to surrender with their followers to the Americans at Pembina. Six was adamantly opposed to this, and replied:

> All the Sioux that wanted to shake hands
> with the Yankees, the Yankees now have; we
> will never make peace with them. They are all
> liars, and this letter [from Major Hatch] you
> now have was written by one of them. Do you
> think I will believe it? And you are a very
> little man to talk to a great chief like me. When
> I want to say anything I say it, and when I
> want to do anything I do it. Nobody can stop
> me!

McKenzie then took another tack. He invited the chief and his friend to his home. Six and Medicine Bottle agreed to go. Then, according to plan, McKenzie endeavored to get them drunk, also using laudanum and chloroform to knock them unconscious. The two were then tied up hand and foot and bound onto sleds. Leaving Fort Garry at eleven o'clock on the 17th, McKenzie arrived with his quarry at Hatch's Pembina stockade on the 18th at twelve noon--they had covered sixty-five miles in thirteen hours. Major Hatch was delighted with his famous prisoners. He wrote to his sister on January 19: "We yesterday had the pleasure of putting irons on the worst Indian in the Sioux nation. One who boasted last spring upon this very ground where he now lies chained, that he had killed some fifteen or twenty white women and children. May his shadow soon be less." Governor Dallas, however, viewed the capture of Little Six as "a very disgraceful proceeding," as the chief "was simply a refugee in our Territory, against whom no complaint had been made officially, and his capture may lead to retaliation."

Sources: Gov. Dallas to Lord Lyons, Feb. 25, 1864, in *Papers Relating to the Hudson's Bay Company's Charter...* (London: Great Britain Colonial Office, 1889), 17-18; J. H. McKenzie and Onisime Giguere, "Capture of Little Six and Grey Iron," printed by Minnesota Legislature, Feb. 1, 1867, 3-10; Alan R. Woolworth, "A Disgraceful Proceeding, Intrigue in the Red River Country in 1864," *The Beaver* (Spring 1969), 54-59; Edwin Hatch to Sister, Jan. 19, 1864, Edwin Hatch Papers, MHS.

"...when I...meet the Americans I will put away my weapons...."

SCARLET PLUME   **February 2, 1864**

AFTER A YEAR AND A HALF of running, Scarlet Plume, the second-ranking chief of the Northern Sissetons, wanted to surrender. He was present for the December 1863 council with Father Andre, but was certain that he was not getting the full story on Sibley's peace proposal. As the winter of 1863-64 progressed, his band went off to hunt buffalo, and the chief was in mourning for the death of his brother, who had been killed by the Americans. In early February Scarlet Plume and Standing Buffalo sent messages to Andre from End of the Woods, on the Assiniboine River. The Metis leader, Jean B. Wilkie, apparently penned the speeches into French. Scarlet Plume stated:

> When you were here, you know I told you
> nothing--not that I did not like the mission
> you represented, but I did not have my own
> people with me, and another thing, I realized
> that all was not told to me, and much concealed,
> and I learned that the talkers were mostly long
> tongues ready to come forward....
>   I am leaving today to get my people....
> When all this affair is over, one way or the
> other, I myself will return to my lands. Your
> interpreters all know me, and my soldier heart
> is strong, and my soldiers will be with me. One
> of the soldiers killed near the fort was my brother--
> he was going to talk to them for the good, and for
> the good he died. I am satisfied, and when I will
> meet the Americans I will put away my weapons--
> they will find my hands clean....I am waiting for
> my people, but they are far away near Devil's Lake--
> I am going to join them. I always did work for
> peace and will continue....

Scarlet Plume eventually surrendered with ten lodges at Fort Wadsworth in November 1864.

Sources: Soldier (Scarlet Plume) to Alexis Andre, Feb. 2, 1864, Belleau Collection, PAM; Diedrich, *Odyssey of Chief Standing Buffalo*, 58-59.

"...you have fed and clothed us from our infancy."

STANDING SOLDIER   **April 20, 1864**

IN THE SPRING OF 1864 eighty chiefs and headmen rode into Fort Abercrombie to surrender to the Americans. Among them were Sweet Corn (chief of the North Island band of Lake Traverse Sissetons), Red Lips (head soldier of Standing Buffalo's band), Makacega (chief of a farmer band), and Standing Soldier (head soldier of the Scarlet Plume band). They explained that they had opposed the hostilities of 1862, but "still have been driven from point to point and have had to live like wolves on the prairie for nearly two years." Furthermore, they had been threatened by the Soldiers' Lodge with death if they left the hostile camps. They had also been told by the Santees at Crow Creek "that it was much better for them to be killed on the open prairies and thus have their sufferings ended," than be confined on the Missouri River and suffer cold and starvation. Despite all of these hindrances to surrender, Standing Soldier concluded:

> **And now we are before you and you have told us the terms upon which we can again be at peace with the Americans, who have fed and clothed us from our infancy, and with whom we have never desired to be at enmity. We have come to take you by the hand because we know you and have confidence in you. We are prepared to do whatever our Great Father through you may require us to do and we will pledge ourselves to conform strictly to the letter of those requirements. We have experienced the difficulties which follow an alienation from those who have always guarded and protected, fed and clothed us, and it makes our hearts glad to see before us a prospect of being able once more to meet the Americans as friends and brothers.**

Standing Soldier and the others were later located near Fort Wadsworth, west of Lake Traverse. He went to Washington in 1867 with others of his tribe and helped in the making of the Great Treaty of 1867 which gave the Santees a reserve in South Dakota, and another at Devil's Lake.

Sources: Joseph Brown to Henry Sibley, April 23, 1864, Department of the Northwest, Letters Received, National Archives, Record Group 393; Diedrich, *Odyssey of Chief Standing Buffalo*, 60.

" We are very anxious to hear from our Mother, the Queen."

SIOUX CHIEFS   August 30, 1864

IN MID—AUGUST 1864 several hundred Sioux arrived at Fort Garry to council with Governor William Mactavish. Among them were the great Sisseton chiefs, Standing Buffalo and Waanatan. They wanted advice and aid from the English. They were under constant threat from American soldiers, and wanted the protection of the Queen. The substance of all the speeches was reported by the newspaper as follows:

> We have here in our camp sixteen medals given to us by our fathers and grandfathers, and we bring them back to the place where our grandfathers got them. They told us that whenever we wanted anything we must come and show these medals to the white people, and from them we would find life.
> Now we find our people spoke the truth. We are very anxious to hear from our Mother, the Queen; we want to know if she has any words for us, and whether she can help us or not, now that we have been driven from our hunting grounds, and we wish to know if there are any troops here to keep the road open between us and you.

Mactavish gave out a few presents to the chiefs, hoping to keep them friendly to the Red River settlers, but he sent them off, preferring that they would make peace with the Americans and remain in American territory.

Sources: *Nor'Wester*, Sept. 1, 1864; Diedrich, *Odyssey of Chief Standing Buffalo*, 64-65.

"Now, if we don't make peace with the Americans, we will spill our blood in Minnesota this summer."

SIOUX CHIEFS   circa April 1865

FOR SEVERAL YEARS following the outbreak of war with the Americans in Minnesota, various bands of eastern Dakotas, as well as Yanktonai, and Teton tribes, continued to run "like wolves" over the northern plains from military expeditions conducted by generals Sibley and Sully. Like Little Crow and Little Six in 1863, and like Standing Buffalo and Waanatan in 1864, the leading Sioux chiefs sought advice and help from the Queen of England. In the past they had been sent away without any solid promises. The chiefs decided once again to appeal to the British by sending a letter to Hypolite Campbell (brother of Antoine J. Campbell), a mixed-blood living at Fort Garry:

> To our Dear Campbell, the blacksmith:
>
> We want to know what the Americans intend to do. We sent three men to a fort on the Missouri to learn whether the Americans would make a treaty, or what they intend doing. But our people have not come back nor have we learned what became of them! Again, we sent off two other messengers to Fort Abercrombie: but there is no word from these either.
>
> There are fourteen hundred tents of us between Devil's Lake and the Missouri alone, and in April next we expect 1,000 Sioux from across the Missouri to join us here at Dog's Tepee. Now, if we don't make peace with the Americans, we will spill our blood in Minnesota this summer. All we wish is, that Sibley would fight like a warrior, when he comes, and not make mud holes and fire at the sky.
>
> We want you to talk with our relations, the Red River people, for us. We call them friends and brothers, because we were always treated well by them. The word of our Grand Mother was always fair and strong; and for that reason we will listen and obey the English in what they tell us.
>
> Try and get some news, and write to us as soon as you can.

Sources: Diedrich, *Odyssey of Chief Standing Buffalo*, 66-67; *Nor'Wester*, April 8, 1865.

TRAVELING HAIL

"...these hills about here are filled with children's graves."

TRAVELING HAIL   September 1865

WHILE MANY EASTERN DAKOTAS had become refugees after the war in Minnesota, the 1,700 that had surrendered fared little better, if not worse. They had been removed from Minnesota by steamboat and shipped to a desolate location on the Missouri River called Crow Creek. Within six months of their arrival on June 1, 1863, some 200 people had died of disease and malnutrition. The rations issued to them in 1864 were pitiful. On December 1, one hundred wagonloads arrived with flour and pork, but the cattle sent were very poor, mostly "skin and bones." By January 1865 the Indians were being fed soup. Three hundred men were allowed to leave the reserve to hunt buffalo, but they had only fifty guns and one pony. Missionary John P. Williamson wrote that many women were "compelled to prostitute their daughters in order to obtain food and clothing." In September 1865, Traveling Hail (who had beaten Little Crow in an election for chief speaker of the Mdewakanton tribe shortly before the war began) told a congressional commission headed by A. W. Hubbard the recent history of his people:

> At Redwood [Oct. --Nov. 1862] they took all the young and smart men and put them in prison, and they took all the chiefs and women and children and put them in Fort Snelling. They done with us as they would grain, shaking it to get out the best, and then brought our bodies over here; that is, took everything from us and brought us over here [Crow Creek] with nothing. Colonel [Clark W.] Thompson stood by us and told us that we would get no more money as annuities, but would get more goods and more to eat. Colonel Thompson...went to Washington and then came back in the winter....[he] told us our goods had been bought and were on the way here; but the goods did not arrive here until the next spring [1864] , and when they did come we thought there were not as many as ought to have come; there were not enough to go around.
>
> ...the agent told us the food was to be divided between us and the Winnebagoes, and only five sacks of flour were given us per week through the winter....They brought beef and piled it up here; they built a box and put the beef in it and steamed it and made soup; they put salt and pepper in it, and that is the reason these hills about here are filled with children's graves; it seemed as though they wanted to kill us.
>
> We have grown up among white folks, and we know the ways of white folks. White folks do not eat animals that die themselves; but the animals that died here were piled up with the beef here and were fed out to us; and when the women and children, on account of their great hunger, tried to get the heads, blood, and entrails, when the butchering was done, they were whipped and put in the guardhouse....
>
> They brought us here to a windy country, and we supposed the wind had blown the goods away; but we heard afterwards that the agent traded some of our goods away....We think if he had not had traded them away there would have been plenty to go around, and the women would not have been crying with cold....
>
> ...we have changed ourselves to white men, put on white man's clothes and adopted the white man's ways...but no one can live here and live like a white man. I have changed my body to a white man's body. I have not told any lie. You told me to tell the truth, and I have done so....

Source: *U.S. Congress Joint Special Committee to inquire into the Condition of the Indian Tribes* (Washington: Government Printing Office, 1867), 406-7. Traveling Hail went to Washington in February 1867, but died the day after his return to the Santee Reserve in Nebraska, on April 25, 1867.

LITTLE SIX

"...over these hills I once rode free on my horse...."

LITTLE SIX and MEDICINE BOTTLE   circa October 1865

NEXT TO LITTLE CROW, White Lodge, and Cut Nose (who was hanged at Mankato), Little Six and Medicine Bottle achieved the most villianous distinction from the whites for their roles in the 1862 war in Minnesota. Little Six had succeeded his father Shakopee as chief only shortly before the war and was considered to be a man of little influence. The Shakopee band in fact split up, with one group following Six's uncle, Red Middle Voice, who camped on Rice Creek. It was members of the Rice Creek faction which began the massacre at Acton on August 17, 1862. Unlike his father, Little Six hated most whites, and he took a prominent part in the killing of women and children. Yet, he apparently did not take an active part in the major battles of the war--Big Eagle said in fact that he never saw Six in a regular fight. Six fled with Little Crow after Wood Lake, but then was kidnapped from British territory, along with Medicine Bottle, in January 1864.

Little Six and Medicine Bottle were both tried by a military court in November 1864, while being confined at Fort Snelling. Six was credited with having warned a man named Joseph Reynolds to escape, and witnesses could not agree on how many people they heard Six say he killed. Medicine Bottle (also called Grey Iron and Black Dog, which were his father's and grandfather's names) was a Soldiers' Lodge leader during the war. He was charged with the murder of Philander Prescott, the old interpreter. His attorney stated, that despite the charges, "No state can reach over into the domain of a foreign and neutral power and drag from its protection any criminal by force." A sentence of death was appealed, but after almost a year of waiting President Andrew Johnson confirmed it (August 29, 1865). Execution of the two leaders was set for November 11. Sometime during his confinement, Six saw a railroad locomotive pass near the fort, and exclaimed to Colonel Robert N. McLaren:

> "Look there--see that--that settles our fate; over
> these lands my father was once undisputed chief,
> and over these hills I once rode free upon my horse,
> and now," pointing to the chain about his waist,
> "look at this," and pointing to the chain running
> from his waist to his foot, "and this" --and scanning
> himself all over, "and these rags."

When Six learned that, after almost two years of confinement, he would be hung, he said:

> I am not afraid to die. When I go into the spirit
> world, I will look the Great Spirit in the face and
> I will tell him what the whites did to my people
> before we went to war. He will do right. I am not
> afraid.

Medicine Bottle, whom some whites wished could be saved, commented:

> I am a man, and have always regarded myself as a
> man. God made me a man and I know I am going to
> die. I have been a warrior since I was eighteen. I have
> fought the Chippewas in twenty battles. I am not
> afraid to again face death.

Sources: *St. Paul Pioneer*, Oct. 14, 1865; Henry B. Whipple, *Lights and Shadows of a Long Episcopate* (New York: Macmillan, 1912), 250-51; William W. Folwell, *A History of Minnesota* (St. Paul: Minnesota Historical Society, 1961), 2:444-50; Woolworth, "A Disgraceful Proceeding," 59. Six's corpse was secretly shipped to Philadelphia where it was displayed at a medical college.

"I never shall have a home until I sleep in the grave."

TAOPI   circa 1866 and February 1869

TAOPI AND A NUMBER OF RELATIVES and friends had been allowed by white authorities to remain in Minnesota after the war of 1862. By 1866, however, Alex Faribault said that the Dakotas could no longer remain on his land, and he asked Bishop Whipple for their removal. It was decided that most of them would be sent to the new Santee Reserve in Nebraska. Whipple held a farewell service for them and the Indians said their last goodbyes. Taopi, however, had been a witness in various trials against his fellow Dakotas, and he feared that the relatives of those who had been hung at Mankato would require his life. He told Whipple:

> My father, I have no blood on my hands, and the Great Spirit knows there is none on my heart. I served your people--I love your Savior--I had a home--I have no home. Taopi cannot go to his people. You hung men at Mankato whose friends will require their blood at my hands. If I go I shall die. I shall never have a home until I sleep in the grave....If I had been a murderer, your people would have fed me in some prison better than an Indian was ever fed by an agent. I am a man, and you leave me to die. I am sick at heart. I have no home. Will you write this to the Great Father?

Whipple did his best to secure some compensation for Taopi, which turned out to be a mere $500.00; yet he was able to get the authorities to allow Taopi to remain in Minnesota. In 1869 Taopi received an offer from the government to live on an eighty acre tract of land on the old reservation. However, by that time, Taopi was on his death bed. He wrote to Whipple:

> I was far beyond St. Paul, but I was sick, so I came to Faribault to see you. I can't walk, so I can't see you. I am getting so I can't hold anything strong, and now if you see my face, you won't see my face plain. While I am a little strong, if you say anything to me, I want to hear it. If you say any word to me when I am dead, I could not hear it.
>
> I am not afraid to die, but I tell you, every man on earth is got to die. You are a bishop and you love every poor man. All the Indians here with me are your friends. I cannot say more, so I shake hands with you.

Taopi died on February 19, 1869--with Whipple at his side. The bishop delivered a funeral sermon for him on March 7, and asked pardon for saying so much for a brother whom he loved.

Sources: Diedrich, "Christian Taopi," 73-76; William Welsh, *Taopi and His Friends* (Philadelphia: Claxton, Remsen, and Haffelfinger, 1869), 53-55.

"All the agents have robbed us!"

WAANATAN, WABASHA, and BIG EAGLE   July 1868

IN THE SUMMER OF 1868 a peace commission met with a number of Sioux chiefs at Fort Rice, Dakota Territory--the commissioners included generals William S. Harney, Alfred H. Terry, and John B. Sanborn. They wanted the chiefs to sign a treaty by which they would agree to settle down on reservations, begin farming, and cede such lands that no longer afforded them game. The Indians chose Joseph LaFramboise as their interpreter. Waanatan, a chief of the Sissetons and Cut Heads of Lake Traverse, who had been roaming the northern plains ever since the war in 1862, said:

> My friends, I am a big man, and my father [Waneta] was also a big man, and you know it. Many years ago when we made treaties with the whites I was told that the country on the other side of the [Missouri] river was ours. My father died when I was quite young [1839-40] ....I was raised on the other side of the river. We never did anything against the whites. I don't want to do anything to the whites, but I see them swarming all over my country.... Take all the whites and your soldiers away and all will be well.
>
> My friends, everything going on here God hears, and I hope nothing wrong will be done. I hope that everything we have been saying will go right straight to our Great Father and that he will hear it. If I could go to see my Great Father I would do it....

Wabasha, the head chief of the eastern Dakotas, spoke to the commissioners on board the steamboat "Agnes," after it left Fort Rice on July 6:

> Ten years ago, when we lived in Minnesota, we threw aside our blankets and strove to live like white men....We saw that the white people lived well, and we determined to try and live like them; hence we have thrown aside the Indian habits and washed the paint off our faces....We have given up all our Indian conjuring and medicine business....We came over to the Missouri [in 1863], and were three years at Crow Creek....We have had an agent....Everything the agent does, he does in confusion.... he makes promises that he never fulfills. We like to live like white people, and consider that an agent ought to be an assistance to us....We do not get enough provisions, though plenty are sent for us....We have had such bad agents that we will not ask for a civilian again, but would like to have a military officer as our agent....All the agents have robbed us!

Big Eagle, who had been imprisoned for three years after the war, added:

> I do not like to speak against our agent behind his back, but I must say that he has kept back from us provisions that came up last year. I have always spoken plainly, and the agent does not like me for doing it. He has even taken boxes of our goods down to Yankton. The stock sent up to us, he keeps at least half of, and makes money from it....

Source: *Papers Relating to Talks and Councils Held with the Indians in Dakota and Montana Territories in the Years 1866-1869* (Washington: Government Printing Office, 1910), 100, 106-8.

"They were chiefs of the mountains and plains...."

STANDING BUFFALO   May 4, 1871

AFTER THE WAR OF 1862, Standing Buffalo and his Northern Sisseton Dakotas
spent some nine years wandering the northern plains, alternately fighting and nego-
tiating with the whites. To survive they followed the buffalo ever westward into
north-central Montana. In the spring of 1871, Standing Buffalo finally decided that
he would make a treaty of peace with the Americans if they would grant his people
an agency and annuity goods. He sent word of his intentions to agent A. Jack Sim-
mons at Fort Browning on Milk River. In his first face to face meeting with an
American official in almost a decade, the chief said that "his heart was good towards
all white people," and that "he spoke with but one tongue." Trader George Boyd
interpreted as Standing Buffalo recounted the postwar history of his people:

> Many years ago they had lived in Minnesota and Dakota
> and on the Missouri below Milk River. Some of them
> knew how to farm, as they had been taught by their white
> fathers. At times they had been friendly and at times at
> war with the whites. They now wanted a long peace. He
> spoke for all his people. They all wanted to shake hands
> and be friends with the white people.
>   Their country below was burnt and dead. The game
> was all gone. They couldn't live in it. They had now come
> here. They liked this country. Here they could make plenty
> of robes and make plenty of meat. Their country was wher-
> ever the buffalo ranged.
>   Here was plenty of buffalo--it was their country and
> they had come to live in it. They were chiefs of the moun-
> tains and plains, they were not poor, but rich, and had
> plenty of horses and robes and wanted to go into the agency
> and trade their robes with the white traders. They would
> shake hands and make permanent peace, but the Great
> White Father must give them flour, coffee, sugar, tobacco,
> and ammunition, and send them blankets, and other things
> as received by the Assiniboines.

Shortly afterwards, Standing Buffalo was goaded into leading a war party against
a large camp of Upper Gros Ventres and Assiniboins. The chief, long tortured
by the adverse circumstances in his life, determined to "throw his body away"
in the battle. True to his word, he charged the enemy (some say without a weapon)
and was killed near the Bearpaw Mountains in early June 1871.

Source: Diedrich, *Odyssey of Chief Standing Buffalo*, 84.

"I will die like my father in the English country."

LITTLE STANDING BUFFALO   February 16, 1874

AFTER THE DEATH OF STANDING BUFFALO, his great following began to
break up. Some returned to Devil's Lake to settle, others eventually remained at
Fort Peck, Montana. However, the chief's son, Bear that Comes and Stands (Mato-
kinajin), or Little Standing Buffalo, took what was left of his father's band north
into the Wood Mountain district of Saskatchewan. He, along with fellow chiefs
White Cap (Wapahaska) and White Eagle (Wamdiska), began to seek aid and a reservation in British territory. In February 1874 the chiefs of the "Wood Mountain
Sioux" attended a council with the lieutenant governor of the Northwest Territories, David Laird, at Fort Qu'Appelle. On that occasion Little Standing Buffalo
spoke of his deceased father, and his intention to remain an "English Indian":

> You see me, I am a boy. I am not able to speak
> like my dead father, but I follow him. My father
> told me to shake hands with the white men and
> die shaking them. I will do what my father told
> me, and my grandfather, he told me the same as
> my dead father....Those are the words of my
> father. He died that way.
> When I go to a place and see the door open,
> I am glad of it. My father never stopped in one
> place. I am the same. When I shake hands with
> the whites and the Crees, I am not afraid; there-
> fore, I travel. I will die like my father in the English
> country. I give half of my body to the whites. I
> would like to go further and further in the north.
> My father told me to go to see the biggest man
> always.

Little Standing Buffalo did not realize that his father had been killed in American
territory, as the line between the two countries had not been physically marked at
that time. Still, the young chief took his father's advice and saw the "biggest men"
in western Canada, and within a few years he was granted a small reserve near
Fort Qu'Appelle. Presently, some five hundred descendants of the Standing Buffalo band live there.

Sources: Minutes of a Meeting held at Qu'Appelle Lakes, Feb. 16, 1874, Alexander Morris Papers, Provincial
Archives of Manitoba, Winnipeg; Diedrich, *Odyssey of Chief Standing Buffalo*, 92-96.

APPENDIX ONE

DAKOTA ORATORS, listed by tribal division:

MANTANTON:

Tiyoskate
Wakantapi

MDEWAKANTON:

Bad Hail
Big Eagle
Big Hunter (Grand Chasseur)
Big Thunder
Cloudman
Grand Partizan
His Bow (or L'Arc)
Little Crow (His Red Nation, Taoyateduta)
Little Six (or Shakopee III)
Medicine Bottle
Petit Corbeau (Little Crow; Hawk that Hunts
          Walking, Chetanwakuamani)
Pinichon (or He That Fears Nothing)
Rattling Runner
Red Owl
Red Wing (or Walking Buffalo)
Shakopee I
Shakopee II (or Standing Cloud)
Tamaha
Taopi
Traveling Hail
Wabasha II
Wabasha III (Bounding Wind)

SISSETON:

Burning Earth
Lean Bear
Little Standing Buffalo (or Bear that
          Comes and Stands, Matokinajin)
Red Iron (or Copper, Mazasha)
Scarlet Plume
Sleepy Eyes
Standing Buffalo
Standing Soldier
Swift Man
Thunder Face
Waanatan
War Eagle that Cries Walking
White Lodge

WAHPEKUTE:

Black Eagle
Cane (Tasagi)
Inkpaduta (Scarlet Point)

WAHPETON:

Akipa
Big Curly Head (or Extended Tail
          Feathers)
Cloudman
Eagle Help
John Other Day
Little Chief
Little Paul Mazakutemani
Mazomani
Rattling Cloud
Running Walker
Spirit Walker
War Club that Shows Itself

APPENDIX TWO

PRINCIPAL INTERPRETERS OF DAKOTA SPEECHES, 1812-1871

Anderson, Thomas., trader and soldier, during the War of 1812

Belland, Henry, Sr., for Little Crow's 1854 trip to Washington, for Flandrau in 1857, and for 1858 Washington trip

Boyd, George., trader, for Standing Buffalo in 1871

Brown, Joseph R., trader and agent, on occasion, late 1850s

Brown, Samuel J., son of J. R. Brown, captive of the Dakotas in 1862

Campbell, Antoine J., son of Scott Campbell, official interpreter for Flandrau 1856-57, for Joseph Brown 1857-58, on 1858 Washington trip, and on occasion afterwards

Campbell, Duncan., brother of Scott Campbell, for Thomas Forsyth 1819

Campbell, Hypolite., brother of A. J. Campbell, blacksmith, 1863 and on at Fort Garry

Campbell, Scott., official interpreter for Lawrence Taliaferro, 1820-40

Crawford, Charles., government employee, on 1858 Washington trip

Dickson, Robert., trader and soldier, during the War of 1812

Dickson (Dixon), William., son of Robert Dickson, 1824 trip to Washington, Nicollet expedition 1839

Faribault, Alexander., trader, for Ramsey 1851-52, for Taopi circa 1863-69

Forbes, William H., trader, for government investigation 1853

Frenier, Antoine D., official interpreter for Brown 1858, and Galbraith 1861-63

Giguere, Onisime., for John McKenzie 1864

Half-breed Charley., for Inkpaduta 1857

Koons, Henry D., for Galbraith 1861

LaFramboise, Joseph, Sr., trader, for Ramsey 1852

LaRocque (Roc, Rock), Joseph., for Nicholas Boilvin, circa War of 1812

Pond, Gideon H., missionary, from the 1830s on, for 1851 treaty negotiations

Pond, Samuel W., missionary, from the 1830s on

Prescott, Philander., official interpreter for agents Amos Bruce, Richard Murphy, Nathaniel McLean, and Murphy again, 1840s through 1857, occasionally afterwards at Redwood Agency

Quinn, Peter., army interpreter and trader, 1850s through 1862

Renville, Gabriel., trader, for William Cullen 1859

Renville, Joseph., official interpreter for the British during the War of 1812, on Stephen Long expedition 1823, and for missionaries at Lac qui Parle till 1846

Riggs, Stephen R., missionary, from the 1830s on

Robertson, Andrew., government employee, on 1858 Washington trip

Robertson, Thomas., son of Andrew Robertson, for Episcopal mission at Redwood 1861-62

Snelling, William J., son of Col. Josiah Snelling, for Long expedition 1823, and on occasion for his father 1820s

Williamson, John P., son of Thomas Williamson, missionary, at Redwood 1861-62, at Crow Creek 1863-65

Williamson, Thomas S., missionary, from the 1830s on

BIBLIOGRAPHY

MANUSCRIPTS

American Board of Commissioners for Foreign Missions Papers, Minnesota Historical Society (MHS), St. Paul
Belleau Collection, Provincial Archives of Manitoba (PAM), Winnipeg
Chauncey Bush Minute Book, Bentley Historical Library, Ann Arbor, Michigan
William Clark Papers, Kansas State Historical Society, Topeka, Kansas
Robert Dickson Papers, MHS
William W. Folwell Papers, MHS
Thomas Forsyth Papers, Missouri Historical Society, St. Louis
Edwin Hatch Papers, MHS
Alexander Morris Papers, PAM
Office of Indian Affairs, microfilm in MHS and National Archives, Washington, Record Group 75
        Documents Relating to Negotiations of Ratified and Unratified Treaties
        with Various Indian Tribes, 1901-1869.

      St. Peter's Agency, Letters Received
      Sioux Claims, Special Files, no. 274
      Special Case 288
Alexander Ramsey Papers, MHS
Thomas Robertson Papers, MHS
Timothy Sheehan Papers, MHS
Alex Siefurt Papers, MHS
Lawrence Taliaferro Papers, MHS
United States War Department, National Archives, Record Group 393
        Department of the North West, Letters Received
Henry B. Whipple Papers, MHS

NEWSPAPERS

Congressional Globe (Washington)
Henderson Democrat
Mankato Weekly Record
Minneapolis State Atlas
Minnesota Democrat (St. Paul)
Minnesota Pioneer (St. Paul)
Minnesota (Weekly and Daily) Times (St. Paul)
Missouri Gazette and Illinois Advertiser (St. Louis)
Niles' (National) Register (Baltimore)
Nor'Wester (Fort Garry, Winnipeg)

St. Cloud Visiter
St. Paul Daily Press
St. Paul Pioneer
St. Paul Pioneer and Democrat
Wabasha Daily Journal

BOOKS AND ARTICLES

Anderson, Gary C. *Kinsmen of Another Kind*. Lincoln: University of Nebraska Press, 1984.
-------------*Little Crow: Spokesman for the Sioux*. St. Paul: Minnesota Historical Society Press, 1986.
-------------"The Removal of the Mdewakanton Dakota in 1837: A Case for Jacksonian Paternalism." *South Dakota History* 10 (Fall 1980):310-33.
Barton, Winifred W. *John P. Williamson: A Brother to the Sioux*. New York: Fleming H. Revell, 1919.
Beltrami, Giacomo C. *A Pilgrimage in America*. 2 vols., London: Hunt and Clarke, 1828.
Blair, Emma H. ed. *The Indian Tribes of the Upper Mississippi Valley....* 2 vols., Cleveland: Arthur H. Clark, Co., 1911.
Bray, Edmund C., and Martha C. Bray, trans. and ed. *Joseph N. Nicollet on the Plains and Prairies*. St. Paul: Minnesota Historical Society Press, 1976.
Brown, Samuel J. "In Captivity," in 56 Congress, 2 session, *Senate Document*, 23 (1900).
Carter, Clarence E. ed. *The Territorial Papers of the United States*. Washington: Government Printing Office, vol. 15, 1951.
Carver, Jonathan. *Travels Through the Interior Parts of North America in the Years 1766, 1767, 1768*. Minneapolis: Ross and Haines, Inc., 1956.
Diedrich, Mark (F.) *The Chiefs Hole-in-the-Day of the Mississippi Chippewa*. Minneapolis: Coyote Books, 1986.
------------"Christian Taopi: Farmer Chief of the Mdewakanton Dakota," *Minnesota Archaeologist* 40 (June 1981):65-77.
------------*Famous Chiefs of the Eastern Sioux*. Minneapolis: Coyote Books, 1987.
------------*The Odyssey of Chief Standing Buffalo*. Minneapolis: Coyote Books, 1988.
------------"Red Wing: War Chief of the Mdewakanton Dakota," *Minnesota Archaeologist* 40 (March 1981):19-32.
------------"Tamaha, 'The One-Eyed Sioux,' One Hundred Years in the Life of a Dakota Medicine Man," an unpublished manuscript, ca. 1982, in Mark Diedrich Papers.
Eastman, Charles A. *Indian Heroes and Great Chieftains*. Boston: Little, Brown, and Co., 1918.
Eastman, Mary H. *The American Aboriginal Portfolio*. Philadelphia: Lippincott, Grambo and Co., 1853.
------------*Dahcotah, or Life and Legends of the Sioux Around Fort Snelling*. New York: Arno Press, 1975.
Flandrau, Charles E. *Recollections of the Past in Minnesota*. St. Paul: Pioneer Press, 1881.
Folwell, William W. *A History of Minnesota*. 4 vols. St. Paul: Minnesota Historical Society, 1921-30.
Forsyth, Thomas. "Journal of a Voyage from St. Louis to the Falls of St. Anthony, in 1819." *Wisconsin Historical Collections* 6 (1872):188-219.
Hargrave, Joseph J. *Red River*. Montreal: John Lovell, 1871.

Heard, Isaac V. D. *History of the Sioux War and Massacres of 1862 and 1863*. New York: Harper and Brothers, 1863.

Holcombe, Return I. and Lucius Hubbard. *Minnesota in Three Centuries, 1655-1908*. 4 vols. Mankato: Publishing Society of Minnesota, 1908.

Holcombe, Return I.ed. "A Sioux Story of the War: Chief Big Eagle's Story of the Sioux Outbreak of 1862." *Minnesota Historical Collections* 6 (1894):382-400.

Hughes, Thomas. *Indian Chiefs of Southern Minnesota*. Minneapolis: Ross and Haines, Inc., 1969.

Keating, William H. *Narrative of an Expedition to the Source of St. Peter's River*. Minneapolis: Ross and Haines, Inc., 1959.

McConkey, Harriet E. *Dakota War Whoop*. St. Paul: D. D. Merrill, 1863.

McKenney, Thomas L. and James Hall. *The Indian Tribes of North America* 3 vols. Edinburgh: J. Grant, 1933.

Minnesota in the Civil and Indian Wars 1861-1865. 2 vols. comp., ed., and pub., under the supervision of the Board of Commissioners for the State. St. Paul: Pioneer Press Co., 1890 and 1893.

Mooney, Michael M. *George Catlin Letters and Notes on the North American Indians*. New York: Clarkson N. Potter Inc., 1975.

Neill, Edward D. "LeSeur, the Explorer of the Minnesota River." *Minnesota Historical Collections* 1 (1872):319-38.

Papers Relating to the Hudson's Bay Company's Charter.... London: Great Britain Colonial Office, 1889.

Parker, Donald D. ed. *The Recollections of Philander Prescott*. Lincoln: University of Nebraska Press, 1966.

Pond, Gideon H. "Dakota Superstition." *Minnesota Historical Collections* 2 (1867):215-55.

Pond, Samuel W. *The Dakotas or Sioux in Minnesota as They were in 1834*. St. Paul: Minnesota Historical Society Press, 1986.

Pond, Samuel W. Jr. *Two Volunteer Missionaries Among the Dakotas*. Boston and Chicago: Congregational Sunday School and Publishing Society, 1893.

Report of the Commissioner of Indian Affairs. Washington: Government Printing Office, 1863.

Riggs, Stephen R. "Dakota Portraits." *Minnesota History Bulletin* 2 (1918):481-568.

-----------*Mary and I: Forty Years with the Sioux*. Boston: Congregational Sunday-School and Publishing Society, 1887.

-----------trans. "Narrative of Paul Mazakootemane." *Minnesota Historical Collections* 3 (1880):82-90.

Robinson, Doane. *A History of the Dakota or Sioux Indians*. Minneapolis: Ross and Haines, Inc., 1956.

Scanlon, P. L. "Nicholas Boilvin, Indian Agent." *Wisconsin Magazine of History* 27 (Dec. 1943):145-69.

Senate Executive Document. no. 61, 33rd Congress, 1 session, 1853-54, serial 699.

Sibley, Henry H. "Sketch of John Other Day." *Minnesota Historical Collections* 3 (1880):99-102.

Snelling, William J. *Tales of the Northwest*. Minneapolis: University of Minnesota Press, 1936.

Taliaferro, Lawrence. "Auto-Biography of Maj. Lawrence Taliaferro." *Minnesota Historical Collections* 6 (1894):189-255.

Tanner, Goerge C. *Fifty Years of Church Work in the Diocese of Minnesota 1857-1907*. St. Paul: Published by the Committee, 1909.

Taylor, Joseph H. "Inkpaduta and Sons." *North Dakota Historical Quarterly* 4 (Oct. 1929-July 1930):152-173.

U.S. Congress Joint Special Committee to inquire into the Condition of the Indian Tribes. Washington: Government Printing Office, 1867.

Wakefield, Sarah F. *Six Weeks in the Sioux Tepees*. Shakopee, Mn.: Argus Book and Job Printing Office, 1864.

Wall, Oscar G. *Recollections of the Sioux Massacre*. Lake City, Mn.: Home Printery, 1908.

Welsh, William. *Taopi and His Friends*. Philadelphia: Claxton, Remsen, and Haffelfinger, 1869.

Whipple, Henry B. "The Civilization and Christianization of the Ojibway." *Minnesota Historical Collections* 9 (1901): 129-42.

-------------*Lights and Shadows of a Long Episcopate*. New York: Macmillan, 1912.

White, Bruce M. "A Skilled Game of Exchange: Ojibway Fur Trade Protocol." *Minnesota History* 50 (Sum. 1987): 229-240.

Winchell, Newton H. *The Aborigines of Minnesota*. St. Paul: Pioneer Co., 1911.

Woolworth, Alan R. "A Disgraceful Proceeding, Intrigue in the Red River Country in 1864." *The Beaver* (Spring 1969):54-59.

Viola, Herman J. *Diplomats in Buckskin, A History of Indian Delegations in Washington City*. Washington: Smithsonian Institution Press, 1981.